Contents

Introduction

On Becoming a Manager in a 21st Century Organization

A city, as I believe, comes into being because each of us isn't self-sufficient but is in need of much.

—*Plato,* Republic *(381 BC)*

We have come to believe and to understand that organizations today are very different from the organizations of the 19th century and, to some extent, even the 20th century. Obviously there have been technological changes in how we make things or serve customers. We use robotics for manufacturing and surgeries. The Pew Research Center survey of U.S. adults found that roughly eight-in-ten Americans are now online shoppers: 79% have made an online purchase, and 51% have bought something using a cellphone.[1] There have also been changes in the expectations of employees and managers. In fact, some of the largest changes in how organizations are structured, managed, and sustained have to do with the roles of managers and employees, as well as how they interact with each other. As the quotation from Plato implies, "we need each other" to make organizations into communities that allow us all to do our best work. Managers, therefore, are community builders.

Before we begin talking about the various roles that managers play, it is worth our time to review how management approaches in organizations have evolved so that we understand better how managerial roles have changed and how they have stayed the same. For those of you reading this book who wish to become a manager someday or who have taken on managerial responsibilities already, knowing why and how your own skills and competencies must continue to grow and develop is vitally important for your success as a manager and leader in all types of organizations. But first, let's discuss how organizational growth and evolution require changes in how organizations are managed.

---

[1] Smith, A. and Anderson, M. (2016). Online shopping and e-commerce. The Pew Research Center. Retrieved from http://assets.pewresearch.org/wp-content/uploads /sites/14/2016/12/16113209/PI_2016.12.19_Online-Shopping_FINAL.pdf, August 12, 2018.

How Organizations Evolve

Most organizations start as entrepreneurial firms. That is, they begin with a person or two having an idea and then deciding to get together and start a business.

Let's imagine for a moment that you and your brother decide to start a little online store. You set up your legal entity (sole proprietorship or LLC), design a website, procure distributors for your inventory, set up the online banking portal to take credit cards or PayPal, and then design ads to begin marketing to the public. But, now, you have to decide which tasks and responsibilities in the online store should be yours and which should be your brother's. Someone has to make sure there is availability of inventory, someone has to pay the invoices for the delivery of the goods, someone has to maintain the website, and someone has to be responsible for marketing your store.

How do you decide who does all that?

For most entrepreneurs, they begin by just divvying up the work based on who likes doing a task or, at least, who is better at it. For example, your brother is really clueless about marketing, so you do it. You hate dealing with customers, wholesalers, and distributors, so your brother does it. In other words, you assign tasks and responsibilities by whoever says, "Okay, I'll do that."

When my wife and I got married she said, "Look, I don't like sweeping floors, and I'm not very good at doing laundry." And I said, "Perfect. I love sweeping floors, and I love doing laundry, but I hate doing dishes and cleaning up the kitchen." So, we began our life together by deciding to do the tasks that we were good at or liked, and we didn't do those that we weren't good at and didn't like.

This same approach works pretty well while you remain a small enterprise; but once a lot more people become employees, you need a better way to organize all the tasks that need done. One approach is to start grouping tasks into those that seem to go together—all the financial tasks, all the maintenance tasks, all the customer service tasks, and so on. In other words, tasks become the foundation for *jobs*. Jobs become the building blocks for the creation of departments; departments become the basis for an organization. Study any organizational chart, and you'll see the pattern. We will talk more about this process in the next chapter.

In an entrepreneurial organization, the owners tend to set the rules, define the policies, hire the people, pay the bills, and do most other tasks themselves. They also set the tone for how to behave professionally and how to treat customers or clients. In fact, the owners establish the way things are done in their organization from the very beginning. This organizational culture defines what it takes to fit in as a member of that organization and, ultimately, how to be successful as an employee or a manager. We will talk more about the role of managers in building and sustaining organizational culture a bit later on.

Once you have multiple people working in multiple jobs, however, the nature of the organization itself changes. As organizations change, though, so do the requirements for managing those organizations. So, let us look for a moment at a few of the more prominent evolutions in management approaches and why they may have occurred.

The Scientific Management Approach

From our earliest times we have produced the bulk of our own food, clothing, furniture, and tools. Up until the late 1700s, most manufacturing was done in homes or small, rural shops (which gave rise to the term, "cottage industries") using hand tools or simple machines. In the late 1700s and early 1800s, however, the invention and continuous improvement of the spinning machine allowed entrepreneurs in craft industries, like textiles and farming, to expand their businesses and enter into what is commonly referred to as the Industrial Revolution period. Industrialization marked a shift to powered, special-purpose machinery, factories, and mass production. It also required more employees to run these machines and produce more goods.

During the early 1900s in these larger, industrial organizations, emphasis started to be placed on the efficiency of machines and increasing the productivity of the people who ran them. That is, owners of these companies needed some way to insure that their investments in people and machinery were being maximized to the fullest. As a result, they needed to hire "agents" to represent their interests. These agents (or, as we now call them, "managers") needed an approach that would maximize the productivity of the workers and machinery, and they adopted principles and practices that we now know as the "scientific management" approach.

Frederick Taylor, who is known as the "father of scientific management," was an engineer who suggested that production efficiency in a factory could be greatly enhanced by eliminating waste in time and motion by employees. Conducting time and motion studies, Taylor showed that standardizing tasks so that they were done only one way and then training employees to do those tasks in that precise way reduced the time spent on the tasks, improved employee productivity, and reduced material waste. He also developed a means of rewarding employees for higher productivity and efficiency that is still used today—the piece rate system.[2] In essence, this system paid

---

[2] Taylor, F.W. (1896). A piece-rate system in *The adjustment of wages to efficiency: three papers on...* The American Economic Association by the Macmillan Company, 89-129.

an incentive on top of regular hourly wages to workers who produced more product in a fixed amount of time.

Taylor thought that if jobs were standardized, employees would become a lot faster at what they did, because they would be doing the same thing over and over. Each employee would have one task and one task only so, theoretically, they would become experts at it.

The unfortunate downside of this approach was that people were treated like machines rather than thinking, creative individuals. Because Scientific Management required a high level of managerial control over employee work practices and entailed a high ratio of managers to employees, it caused some friction between workers and managers. Criticisms commonly came from workers who were subjected to an accelerated work pace, lower product quality, and lagging wages. Though Scientific Management often has been opposed by employees, its value in streamlining production was indisputable and its impact on the development of mass production techniques immense.[3]

One of the unintended consequences of the Scientific Management approach was that unions became stronger to protect the rights of workers from the uncontrolled power wielded by managers. Ironically, the very reason factory owners wanted to adopt the approach was to maximize their financial investments. But unionization actually caused owners to have less control, to have to pay higher wages, to be required to invest more in factory safety, and generally have their profits reduced. In response, our next major managerial evolution went in the opposite direction and advocated treating workers more like humans rather than machines.

The Human Relations Approach to Management

The human relations theory of management developed in the early 1920s shortly after Taylor's death. Managers adopting this approach believe that people desire to be part of a supportive team that facilitates development and growth. Therefore, if employees are encouraged to participate, use and develop their skills, and perceive their work has significance, then they are motivated to be more productive, which generally results in higher quality work.

In the forefront of the Human Relations movement was Elton Mayo, a professor at the Harvard Business School, who conducted a series of experiments over several years that were designed to focus on what employees needed, what they wanted, and their need for autonomy and decision making ability over their own lives and jobs. He discovered that how employees are treated in their

---

[3] Taylor, F.W. (1911). *Principles of scientific management*. New York, London, Harper & Brothers.

organizations really determines how successful the organization will be in the long term.[4] Mayo recognized the "inadequacies of existing scientific management approaches" to industrial organizations, and underlined the importance of relationships among people who work for such organizations.[5]

From a management perspective, the Human Relations approach required much more social and emotional connection between managers and their employees. Specifically, managers who understand the nature of informal ties among workers can make significantly better decisions for both the organization and the employees. Mayo concluded that people's work performance is dependent on both social relationships and job content.

Fast-forward 100 Years ....

Although most of the original theories of management (and there were a LOT) emerged in the 19th and 20th centuries, those of you reading this book are more interested in what successful organizations require now and in the future. In other words, what do 21st century organizations require of managers today and tomorrow?

This question forms the basis for the chapters to follow. Our approach will be that no matter which organization(s) you work for in your management career, each will require you to adopt several roles. It is those roles for which you must prepare yourselves. That is, no matter how much organizations change, they will always require managers to make decisions, solve problems, engage employees, lead change, mediate and resolve conflicts, coach and develop talent, and evaluate performance. And while it is true that employees will be involved more and more in some of these roles, managers will always be needed to move organizations forward to places they do not realize they need to go!

What's Next?

In the next chapter we look first at how managers "see" organizations. That is, we will discover that every manager uses different lenses to analyze, design, lead, and manage organizations, departments, and employees. You will likely discover that you have a preference for one such lens, but the challenge is to practice using all three to give yourself the best possible information as you become a manager.

So let's get started!

---

[4] Mayo, E. (1933). *The human problems of an industrial civilization*. Cambridge, MA: Harvard.

[5] Miner, J.B. (2006). *Organizational behavior, Vol. 3: Historical origins, theoretical foundations, and the future*. Armonk, NY and London: M.E. Sharpe.

Understanding Your Organization

In the successful organization, no detail is too small to escape close attention.

—Lou Holtz, former University of Notre Dame head football coach

One of the most important responsibilities of managers is to understand the organizations that employ them. Although it is likely that most organizations have a number of very similar aspects, every organization is unique in how it is organized and how it gets things accomplished. In this chapter, we will examine three different "lenses" that managers can use to analyze and understand the inner workings of their organizations: the strategic design lens, the political lens, and the cultural lens.[1] Each of these ways of viewing organizations provides a different perspective that can guide how we enact all the roles that we play as managers. Before we examine each of these lenses in detail, it will be helpful to understand how each of us brings our own personal viewpoints and biases to our management roles. By understanding our own preferred way of seeing the world, we can learn to incorporate different views of our organizations using multiple perspectives or "lenses."

Understanding Our Own Schemas

Social psychologists have termed the way individuals cognitively organize the world as *schemas*. We all have schemas in which our past experiences are organized into mental structures that allow us to quickly retrieve relevant and familiar information. As we experience certain situations or are presented with the same data over and over again, rather than rethink each situation anew, it is easier for us to react in the same ways we have done in the past.

---

[1] Ancona, D., Kochan, T., Maureen, S., Van Maanen, J., & Westney, E. (1996, 1999, 2005). *Managing for the future: Organizational behavior and processes* (1–3 eds.). South-Western College Publishing.

In essence, *schemas are shortcuts that help us make decisions.* We all have multiple schemas that we've developed over our lifetimes, everything from which route minimizes the time it takes to get to work to the systematic way we go through the grocery store. When new information is presented to us, these mental models provide us with a quicker path to understand and interpret the new information and, ultimately, to make decisions.

The development of schemas in organizations is equally helpful, so that new tasks, projects, or events don't require that we start from scratch every time. This is one of the benefits of having longer-tenured, experienced employees and managers in the organization. They have developed schemas for getting things done quickly and avoiding the pitfalls or barriers many newer folks would stumble into.

Unfortunately, schemas have their downsides, too. Over time, schemas can develop into stereotypes, biases, and prejudices. Moreover, they don't just reflect what is going on at the moment but also act to perpetuate such biases into the future.

Consider the issue of whether an organization should use employee referrals to find new employees. One of the manager's schemas might be that "our current successful employees will refer more excellent employees to us." And while this may be true at some level, it is also true that employees tend to refer others who are just like them.[2] Therefore, using employee referrals as the primary source of new employees is likely to perpetuate having a staff with identical interests and talents, as well as similar prejudices and biases, resulting in less diversity of talents, ideas, and experiences.

Another challenge posed by schemas is that when we receive new data or experience new situations, we tend to make them "fit" our existing schemas, even if they present contradictory information. The most common reaction is to simply ignore or quickly forget the new information.[3] In fact, sometimes an individual does not even perceive the new information, or they interpret the new information in ways that minimize how much they must change their schemas. As a result, our set of preconceived ideas and mental scripts are difficult to change once they are established.

---

[2] Kristof-Brown, A. L. (2000). Perceived applicant fit: Distinguishing between recruiters' perceptions of person-job and person-organization fit. *Personnel Psychology, 53*(4), 643–671.

[3] Taylor, S. E., & Crocker, J. (1981). Schematic bases of social information processing. In E. T. Higgins, C. A. Herman, & M. P. Zanna (Eds.), *Social cognition: The Ontario Symposium on Personality and Social Psychology* (pp. 89–134). Hillsdale, NJ: Lawrence Erlbaum.

A good example of this is the movement known as the "Flat Earth Society," which is made up of members who believe that the Earth is a flat sphere bounded by ice.[4] Even when shown satellite images taken by astronauts and showing Earth as a sphere, the members of this society attribute Earth's curvature to the use of a wide-angle camera lens or "photo-shopped" pictures. So, even in the face of actual photographs and scientific data, the members' schema interpret the data in ways that confirm their own biased view.

We see this in organizations, too. For example, sociology research has shown that women in science are deemed to be inferior to men and are evaluated as less capable when performing similar or even identical work. In a recent study, even when presented evidence to the contrary, male STEM faculty assessed the quality of real research that demonstrated bias against women in STEM as being low; instead, the male faculty favored fake research, designed for the purposes of the study in question, which purported to demonstrate that no such bias exists.[5] In other words, the male science faculty's schema interpreted the research that supported their preconceived notions, even when that research was fake.

Because they are difficult to change, schemas also pose a great challenge when change is required. Remember that people develop schemas to help them cope with and avoid problems within their organizations. When organizations experience change, it requires employees and managers to develop new schemas to address new problems and challenges, and that takes a lot of energy and attentiveness! As a result, people resist changes much of the time, because they really don't want to expend the mental energy to change their approaches and their schemas.

Finally, schemas are never complete. We form our mental models over time, so the assumptions we make about why something happens—our causal reasoning—may be incorrect. Here's a funny story about a newlywed couple that demonstrates the notion that we often attribute cause to a behavior or a decision due to a completely incorrect assumption:

Sally wanted to make Bob, her new husband, his favorite dinner: baked ham. So she visited her mother-in-law to ask for the recipe she knew Bob loved. Her mother-in-law proceeded to read her the recipe, which Sally dutifully wrote down until she got to this part: "Cut off the butt end of the ham and place in roaster." Sally, wanting to make sure she understood the

[4]The Flat Earth Society. https://www.tfes.org/
[5]Handley, I. M., Brown, E. R., Moss-Racusin, C. A., & Smith, J. L. (2015). Gender-biased evaluations of gender-bias evidence. *Proceedings of the National Academy of Sciences*, October 2015, 112, 43, 13201–13206; doi:10.1073/pnas.1510649112

directions correctly asked, "Why do you do that?" Her mother-in-law said, "Actually, I have no idea. This was my mother's recipe, and I've always followed the recipe and done it. Let's call her and find out." So they called Bob's grandmother and asked her about that part of the directions. She laughed heartily for a moment, and then said, "Because my pan wasn't big enough for the whole ham!"

As you can plainly see, there are benefits and drawbacks with schemas. While they are extremely helpful to us as managers, they do require us to examine our assumptions and our own personal biases and prejudices. An important part of becoming an effective 21st-century manager is to develop multiple perspectives on organizations. In the following sections, we will examine three different approaches to analyzing our organizations so that we can test our assumptions about why things happen and which approaches to leading change, making decisions, dealing with problems, and engaging employees might be the most helpful to us in specific situations.

The Strategic Design Lens

Managers who "see" the organization through a strategic design lens view the organization's primary function as achieving goals in the most effective and efficient way possible. We use the term *effectiveness* to mean that the organization is achieving its goals at the level needed to be successful over the long term ("doing the right things"). When we use the term *efficiency,* we mean that the organization is achieving its goals by deploying the least resources possible, that is, time, money, people ("doing things right").

A manager whose preferred schema is strategic design also recognizes that how the organization is designed and structured should match the overall strategy of the firm. Moreover, to be highly effective the organization's strategy and design must be compatible with the environment within which the organization operates. For example, a small furniture manufacturer that faces a number of larger competitors may decide to focus its strategy on making premium, one-of-a-kind chairs for a smaller niche market, rather than trying to compete with the larger firms on cost. In essence, it has a low-volume, high-cost strategy. Therefore, to be structured to match that strategy, it may be organized around teams of employees that make each chair by hand, unlike its larger competitors with a high-volume, low-cost strategy that have assembly lines of employees assembling standardized chair parts.

What Are Strategic Design Managers "Looking" for?

Managers who primarily view their organizations through a strategic design lens might begin by asking, "What are we trying to achieve?" In essence this question asks about the organization's goals. These can be *terminal goals* (desired end results or the "what") about product or service quality, quantity sold, product delivery times, rank among competition, market share, stock price, accumulation of capital, employee success, and other outcomes the senior leadership in the organization wants to achieve. They can also be *process goals* (the behaviors or the "how"), such as decision-making approaches, use of teams, diversity and inclusion, creativity and innovation, and other ways of doing things. Process goals are typically the means used to achieve the terminal goals.

Once these are clarified, the next question becomes, "What tasks are required to achieve the organization's goals?" It is important to look at all the tasks required, because tasks are the basic building blocks of any organization. Some tasks are very simple, and some are very complex. Some tasks can be done in any order, and some must be done sequentially. Some tasks require a lot of resources, and some require very few. From a management perspective, however, the key is to know exactly which tasks need to be done, when they need to be done, and which skills, talents, and resources are needed to do them.

Once the tasks are identified, the next question managers need to answer is, "How should all the required tasks relate to each other effectively enough to implement the organization's strategy?" This next step helps managers decide how tasks should be grouped together to form jobs. Understanding the nature of skill requirements, the amount and type of resources required, and the level of task complexity helps managers know how all the tasks relate to each other across the organization. In strategic design language, this is known as *strategic grouping*. The decision to group certain tasks together and call them a "job" requires the manager to understand the relationships among the tasks and then to group them together according to their similarity. As an example, in thinking about all the different tasks required to perform accounting in a large organization, it is usual to group tasks together that require taking in money ("Accounts Receivable" job) separately from tasks that require paying out money ("Accounts Payable" job). In a very small firm, however, all accounting tasks may be grouped together into one job called "Accountant."

Sometimes, like in our accounting example, strategic grouping is by *function*, such as accounting, marketing, sales, human resources, production, and so on. This grouping approach is very common, but there are other grouping approaches that may make more sense for some organizations.

Firms with multiple brands, products, or services often group jobs based on each individual brand, product, or service. A good example of this is General Motors, which has multiple car brands (e.g., Chevrolet, Buick, Cadillac, GMC), yet each brand has its own marketing, human resources, finance, and manufacturing jobs, as well as its own senior management team that oversees that brand. The advantage to this *product* grouping structure is that each brand has a clear understanding of the financial costs and profits required to operate successfully. When a brand isn't doing well, it can be discontinued or sold off without negatively affecting the rest of the organization. GM, for example, discontinued Pontiac and Saturn because they were not profitable. Likewise, Proctor and Gamble sold most all of its pet food brands in 2014 because it wanted to focus solely on personal brands and cleaning products.[6] In addition, because the market focus is different for each brand (e.g., Cadillac is marketed to those higher in socioeconomic status while Chevrolet is targeted to those in lower socioeconomic markets), managers can focus their organizing, staffing, marketing, advertising, and other areas more strategically.

Another grouping option, particularly for large multinational organizations, is to structure by *geography*. This would allow them to have divisions that are geographically close to suppliers or customers in Europe, Asia, North America, or South America, for example. Each location is overseen by a team of managers who have responsibility for the entire operation and its finances. Geographic organizational structure allows for each business unit or office to operate as its own entity based on where it's located.

Organizations that have different types of customers may choose to structure based on *customer* or *market* type, such as insurance companies that serve commercial, auto, life, property, or other customer lines. These organizations have different products or services based on customer or market segment, and this structure allows more effective and efficient marketing, sales, logistics, and general knowledge of what each customer or market wants or needs. The point is that strategic grouping should make sense based on the strategic intention of the firm, what it is trying to accomplish (goals),

---

[6] Wahba, P. (2014, April 9). P & G selling petfood brands to mars for $2.9 billion, *Reuters*, Business News.

direct reports of its own, too. Note that the marketing assistant has no direct reports, but reports directly to the VP. The strategic linking of these positions shows with whom information should be shared and who must provide resources to whom.

However, this formal arrangement doesn't actually provide practical linking mechanisms so that each area of marketing can communicate with the other in an efficient way. Without some sort of informal liaison roles assigned that are able to cross the boundaries between the more formal roles, organizations find that they operate in "silos." You are probably familiar with grain silos that farmers use to separate different types of grain. In organizations, silos represent artificial barriers that separate different types of employees. When employees interact poorly with people outside of their "silo," it becomes difficult to carry out business operations. A tight-knit department that works well together is great, but organizational silos can be like fortresses within a company and eventually cause serious problems in communication and teamwork.

In the previous example of the marketing department structure, it might be wise to have someone from both Brand X and Brand Y product development sit in on the monthly sales meeting so that customer feedback is known first-hand to those responsible for designing product packaging. These informal liaison roles can then take back the information to the product development team and manager so that any new designs or redesigns of the packaging reflect the information gleaned from the sales reps' interactions with customers.

There are many ways to link information, resources, and people together to ensure that the strategy and structure of an organization is efficient and effective, as well as making sure that the designed (or redesigned) organization fits into the environment in which it operates. But there is one more question that managers need to consider as they view business processes and performance through the strategic design lens:

"Do the rewards and incentives we provide support the behaviors that need to occur to achieve the organization's strategies and goals?"

Aligning Rewards

There is nothing more frustrating for a manager than to have people working against the strategy or to have them competing against each other's goals. But this happens very frequently due to misaligned performance measures as well as unintentionally providing employees with competing rewards and incentives. Therefore, the third aspect of the strategic design process is all about *strategic alignment*.

and the efficiency and effectiveness of getting its products and servic
customers.

In whatever way the organization is strategically grouped, the next
cision a manager must make is to ensure that information and resou1
that are needed can be shared across the organization efficiently and eff
tively. This part of strategic design is known as *strategic linking*. One of t.
most common ways to organize information flow and job responsibilities
through constructing an *organizational chart*.

The Organizational Chart

As a visual representation of how jobs are strategically linked, a company's
organizational chart provides a clear roadmap of who is responsible for ensuring that information flows to who needs it, as well as outlining the hier-
archy of reporting relationships. Consider the following very brief depiction
of a functional grouping in Marketing:

You will notice that each of the management "jobs" listed—sales manager, advertising manager, and product development manager—are direct
reports to the VP of marketing. Each of these positions has one incumbent
and specific responsibilities, and each is different from the other. Each has

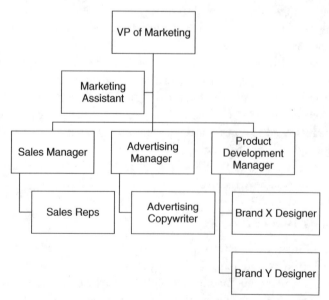

Figure 1 Example of Functional Grouping in Marketing

Source: Dale J. Dwyer

Consider an organization that makes chairs and has a high-volume, low-cost strategy. The production employees are rewarded for making sure they produce a lot of chairs without any wasted resources, and, subsequently, each member of the production department (including the manager) earns bonuses when the company achieves a high profit margin on the chairs. As a result, the motivation for the production department and its managers is to keep costs low and produce lots of saleable chairs.

Conversely, the sales representatives are rewarded based on the number of chairs they sell—the more they sell, the more money they make. Therefore, the motivation for the sales reps is to keep the price as low as possible so that they sell more chairs than their competition. But if they negotiate a lower price of the chairs with customers so that their sales volume increases, it results in a lower profit margin and, thus, the production employees lose their bonus (or, at least, part of it). In essence, sales reps' incentives to sell more chairs at a lower price actually incentivizes the production team to reduce costs to keep its profit margin as high as possible so bonuses don't suffer. These reductions might be in the form of using cheaper materials, cutting back on quality inspections, or downsizing the production line.

See the problem?

The two internal departments—sales and production—have competing goals and, more importantly, are rewarded for pursuing these incompatible goals.[7] When an organization has such misalignment, the benefits of its strategic design are lost. Remember: people do what they are rewarded for doing, a subject we will address more fully in Chapter 7.

Using the Strategic Design Lens

As a manager, your primary task is to make sure that people have the skills, training, resources, and information to do the jobs they were hired to do. But another part of your job is to keep asking questions and then working to bring people, policies, practices, and performance into alignment:

- "What strategies and structures work best to make sure that we attain our goals?" In the fast pace of most 21st-century organizations, this is not a one-and-done question but requires continual coordination and realignment. For example, if senior management decides to expand the product line or to build a new market in Asia, they must adopt new marketing

---

[7] This classic article discusses the phenomenon of having misaligned goals and rewards: Kerr, S. (1995). On the folly of rewarding A while hoping for B. *The Academy of Management Executive, 9*(1), 7–14.

strategies as well as develop a new structure that involves increased production capacity and distribution channels.

- "How can I make sure that my employees know and understand the goals and strategies?" This requires the ability to explain complex strategies so that everyone understands WHY they are doing what they're doing, not just complying with the managers' directions.
- "Which rewards and incentives should I use to ensure that employees and managers are motivated to engage in behaviors that we truly want and not ones that we don't want?"[8]

Ultimately, managers who view their organizations through a strategic design lens see them as rational systems that can be designed such that goals are set, problems and challenges to those goals are clearly identified, and the means used to circumvent those challenges and achieve those goals are effective and efficient. As such, it is a rather impersonal view of management. Managers who only see the organization as a series of goals to be achieved, strategies to be devised, structures to be designed, and rewards to be aligned tend to miss some of the other, more person-centered aspects of what makes an organization tick, as we will see in the descriptions of the other two lenses.

The Political Lens

One of the more interesting ways that managers view organizations, and some would say one of the more negative ways, is as a political system that is rife with conflict and internal competition for resources. That said, managers who view the organization through a political lens might ask, "How can I use power and influence, negotiation, and coalition-building to achieve our goals?" To begin studying the political lens, we first need to understand some basic principles and sources of power and interests.

What Are Authority, Power, and Influence?

How does an organization develop into an arena requiring political navigation? One aspect has to do with how power is viewed, used, and negotiated. As a starting point, let's look at the differences between three concepts that are often used interchangeably, but are quite different: *authority*, *power*, and *influence*.

Authority is usually associated formally with a position, not a person. Managers, just by virtue of their position, generally are given some authority

---

[8] Kerr, S. (1975). On the folly of rewarding A while hoping for B." *Academy of Management Journal, 18*(4), 769–783.

to make decisions in their units. For example, the VP of marketing has formal authority to hire and supervise people, as well as to allocate resources, by virtue of the position itself, and it doesn't matter who the actual person is in that role. Most people who are subordinate to a position's formal authority recognize it and, regardless whether they like the person in the position or not, they generally follow directions, assignments, and requests given by that person.

When dealing with legitimate authority, the position itself has power vested in it, even if the actual individual in the position doesn't have personal power or influence. Consider the Office of President of the United States. By virtue of Article II of the Constitution, the Office of President has the power to sign treaties and grant pardons. But depending on who actually is President of the United States at the time, they may face resistance in signing a treaty or granting a pardon from those who don't like or approve of the person who holds the office.

Jeffery Pfeffer, a noted scholar on power and politics, defines *power* as "the potential ability to influence behavior, to change the course of events, to overcome resistance, and to get people to do things that they would not otherwise do."[9] Notice his use of the phrase "potential ability." That implies that even if we are able to accrue power, we may not necessarily use it.

Again, consider the President of the United States. If we like who holds the office, we tend to trust them when it comes to policy decisions, cabinet appointments, or other executive actions. The President, knowing this, may choose to capitalize on that personal power by not taking a controversial action and, as a result, end up accruing more power. In other words, the President has the authority, as well as the potential ability (the power), to change something, but may decide not to exercise that power.

If we think of power as the source of our ability to get people to do something, we can think of *influence* as the actual use of power to persuade them to do it. Just as electric power that is ever-present in your home can light a lamp only if the lamp is plugged into the source of the power, as managers our influence or effectiveness is dependent on our source of power and how we wield it.

Besides the power flowing from the legitimate authority we hold, the source of our personal power generally falls into at least one of five categories[10]:

---

[9] Pfeffer, J. (1992). *Managing with power: Politics and influence in organizations* (p. 90). Boston, MA: Harvard Business School Press.

[10] French, J. R. P., & Raven, B. (1959). The bases of social power. In D. Cartwright and A. Zander (Eds.), *Group dynamics*. New York, NY: Harper & Row.

1. Informational—the extent to which we have information that others want or need to know
2. Expertise—the extent to which others believe we are knowledgeable about an area or subject
3. Referent—the extent to which others want to be like us or have affiliation with us
4. Reward—the extent to which we are able to offer a desirable reward to others for gaining their compliance
5. Coercive—the extent to which we are able to gain compliance from others by issuing a threat of negative outcomes.

As managers, we want to avoid using reward and coercive power, since these only gain compliance or maintain one's control over others for a short period of time. Rather, power that accrues to us through having information, being seen as an expert in an area, or being someone others want to be like or be with tends to be more effective in the long-run at instituting changes, building coalitions, and engaging in substantive decisions that affect people and organizations.

Individual versus Collective Interests

Of course, all the authority, power, and influence in the world will not work to get someone to voluntarily do something unless they believe it is in their best interests to do so. *Interests* refer to what is at stake for people affected by a decision or action. In other words, how a decision or an action benefits them or hurts them will determine whether they support it or oppose it. Most of us tend to support management decisions that benefit us and oppose those that we believe are not in our best interests. That is why, as a manager, it is important to recognize what is at stake for all of the employees affected by our decisions and actions.

In addition to thinking about how something affects us individually, as members of an organization (or a department or a team), we usually identify with the collective interests of that group. In the marketing department organizational chart that we discussed earlier, it is likely that all employees share some common interests in obtaining resources, being productive, and sharing in each other's success. But in most organizations, there are many ways that the individual and collective interests of one group may be at odds with those of other individuals or groups.

Consider the very basic makeup of demography (age, sex, race, marital status, etc.) in an organization that can be affected differently by management decisions on health care benefits, telecommuting, technology, or mentoring. Working parents may be affected positively by having the opportunity to work from home. LGBTQ employees may be affected negatively by the organization's decision not to offer domestic partner benefits.

Groups may wield collective power differently, too. Older employees often use the power of their experience and expertise in a positive way to influence or mentor younger employees, while the younger employees may use the power of their technological prowess to create new and more efficient ways to work.

The management challenge is to analyze those individual and collective interests and then decide how to weigh the priority of them for all the stakeholders in the decision. In addition, a manager must also understand how much power and influence those stakeholders have to oppose or support decisions or actions. Learning how to leverage the power and interests of others to create change, establish coalitions of employees so decisions are implemented, and achieve organizational goals is the mark of a good "manager as politician."

Critical Resources as a Source of Power

One way to think of power is the ability to control critical resources or to provide scarce and valuable knowledge or expertise.[11] The person or unit in an organization whose expertise, knowledge, or resources can be brought to bear on a critical problem the organization faces accrues power with other people or units. For example, in an organization faced by product liability suits, the legal team gains power because of its expertise. When an organization is trying to increase its market share, the sales force accrues power the more it sells. Notice, too, that power in the organization shifts depending on what critical resource or expertise is required in the moment. That, of course, makes managers' jobs more complex, because they have to recognize what is needed, when it is needed, and who can provide it.

Using the Political Lens

As a manager who views the organization as areas of conflict that must be negotiated between and among stakeholders, the ability to recognize who will be affected by what you intend to do, the prioritizing of their interests, and the recognition of who will support you and who will oppose you is crucial to

---

[11] Salancik, G. R., & Pfeffer, J. (1977). Who gets power—and how they hold on to it: A strategic-contingency model of power. *Organizational Dynamics, 5*(3), 2–21.

being able to navigate the political machinations that will occur. Pfeffer suggests four questions that need to be answered as you proceed[12]:

1. Whose support *must* you have to move the decision or action forward?
2. Who are the stakeholders affected by the decision or action (directly or indirectly)?
3. Who is so opposed to the decision that they could completely derail the action?
4. Who could be a part of a coalition of supporters who will help implement the decision, and what are their interests in seeing it succeed?

Answering these questions helps managers to do several things in order to get decisions implemented: analyze the location of power and influence, figure out who is affected and how, build a coalition of supporters, get buy-in from those who may oppose the decision, and negotiate so that the collective interests of the organization are perceived to be stronger than any individual or subgroup interests.

No easy task! But a skilled "manager as politician" will be seen as someone who can get things done, overcome opposition, and build relationships across boundaries. It is very important that you develop these skills so that you can navigate the myriad political problems that stand in the way of achieving the goals of your organization and your department.

In the next section, we'll look at the third lens that managers use to understand the ways in which organizational members create meaning for what they do and how they do it. Although it may be less rational in managing organizations than the strategic design lens or even the political lens, it is a rich source of information that managers can use to understand "how things get done" in their companies so that they are able to achieve the organization's goals.

The Cultural Lens

The basis for a cultural perspective on organizations comes from anthropology—the study of societies and their cultures. Like a society, organizational culture is acquired through socialization and enculturation of employees. As Conrad Phillip Kottak writes, "Enculturation is the process where the culture that is currently established teaches an individual the accepted norms and values of the culture or society where the individual lives. The individual can

---

[12] Pfeffer, J. (1992). *Managing with power: Politics and influence in organizations.* Boston, MA: Harvard Business School Press.

become an accepted member and fulfill the needed functions and roles of the group. Most importantly the individual knows and establishes a context of boundaries and accepted behavior that dictates what is acceptable and not acceptable within the framework of that society."[13]

Managers who tend to see their organizations as mini societies or cultures usually ask this question: "How do the cultural elements (e.g., the stories, myths, symbols, artifacts, values) that define our organization help me to understand and better manage employees' attitudes and behaviors?" Culture also influences how we attempt to align the cultural elements with organizational goals and strategies. Moreover, we begin to realize the important role that we and our employees have in shaping the organization's culture.

To get a clearer picture of what is involved in an organizational culture, we need to understand all the things that contribute to a strong culture. Like the anthropologist, we call these aspects *cultural artifacts*. In anthropology, artifacts are created by the people of the society to demonstrate or symbolize their culture. Studying artifacts can help us know what that society and culture were like when they existed. For example, some of the earliest ceramic pottery discovered in Upper Mesopotamia (modern-day Iraq, Turkey, and Syria) was highly decorated with symbols and art. The pottery was thought to be used just for storing food. But after studying the pottery and understanding what the symbols and art stood for, archeologists determined that the pottery was used primarily for cooking and serving food during special occasions, such as religious festivals or weddings.[14]

In organizational life, there are many types of cultural artifacts that can help us know what the organization is like to work for. Here are just a few examples, taken from the classic 1982 book by Deal and Kennedy,[15] in which they suggested that the basis of corporate culture was an interlocking set of six cultural elements:

- **History**—A shared narrative of the past lays the foundation for corporate culture. The accepted traditions of the past keep people anchored to the core values that the organization was built on. Conversely, invented

---

[13] Kottak, C. P. (2008). *Window on humanity: A concise introduction to anthropology.* New York, NY: McGraw-Hill.

[14] Nieuwenhuyse, O. P., Akkermans, P. M. M. G., & Plicht, J. (2010). Not so coarse, nor always plain—the earliest pottery of Syria. *Antiquity, 84,* 71–85.doi:10.1017/S0003598X00099774

[15] Deal, T. E., & Kennedy, A. A. (1982). *Corporate cultures: The rites and rituals of corporate life.* Reading, MA: Addison-Wesley.

traditions can be seen as attempts to produce a common identity where none previously existed.

- **Values and beliefs**—Cultural identity is formed around the shared beliefs of what is really important and the values that determine what the organization stands for.
- **Rituals and ceremonies**—Ceremonies are the things that employees do every day that bring them together. Examples include Friday afternoon get-togethers or simply saying goodbye to everyone before you leave for the day. They can also include more formal rituals, such as celebrations of organizational or individual milestones.
- **Stories and myths**—Corporate stories typically exemplify company values and capture dramatically the exploits of employees who personify these values in action. Stories allow employees to learn about what is expected of them and better understand what the business stands for.
- **Heroes**—These are the employees and managers whose status is elevated because they embody organizational values. These heroes serve as role models and their words and actions signal the ideal to aspire to. Stories employees tell often include heroes and their actions.
- **The cultural network**—The informal network within an organization is often where the most important information is learned. You might have heard the saying, "there are no secrets in organizations," and this is primarily because of the following characters who are a part of the organization's cultural network:
  - *Storytellers*, who interpret what they see happening and create stories that can be passed on to initiate people to the culture.
  - *Gossipers*, who put their own spin on current events and feed people a steady diet of interesting information. Employees know not to take the information at face value; however, they enjoy the entertainment value of a gossip story.
  - *Whisperers*, who have the ear of the powerful people in the organization. They can be used by anyone with a message they want taken to the top. Whisperers generally don't want to use formal communication channels.
  - *Spies*, who provide valuable information to top management and let the management know what really happens on a daily basis.
  - *Priests/priestesses*, who are the guardians of cultural values and the "confessors" of the organization. They know the history of the company inside out and can be relied on to interpret a current situation using the beliefs, values, and past practices of the company. They are also who others go to when they have an interpersonal or process grievance.

The basic idea behind seeing an organization through a cultural lens is that organizations are social societies that must work together, collectively, to accomplish the goals and live out the mission of the whole organization. Therefore, if managers can identify and interpret correctly each of the cultural elements that distinguish the organization, they will be able to avoid making cultural errors in managing their meaning.

Using the Cultural Lens

Managers who view the organization through a cultural lens can develop a rich understanding of why things are done the way they are and how people "learn" the culture. In addition, from a manager's perspective, understanding culture permits strategies to be developed that help shape the culture toward the goals and outcomes that senior leaders desire for the organization. To that end, there are several actions you can take that can help guide how culture can be shaped to support the mission, vision, goals, and strategies:

- Walk around your organization and notice these symbols.
  - Posters, pictures, and plaques. What do they represent about what your organization values? What might they tell visitors about your company?
  - Office arrangements. How are offices arranged? Are there cubicles that separate people from each other? Are employees in an open area, with little separation? Are managers' offices separate with walls and doors? What messages are conveyed by the office arrangements—are they welcoming or send the message, "don't bother me"?
  - Reception area(s). Do they convey a sense of openness and welcome? Are they comfortable? Keep in mind that large, open areas with comfortable chairs, TV monitors, books/magazines, and refreshments signal that visitors may be waiting awhile!
- Talk to longer-tenured members of your organization. Ask them to name someone who typifies the core values of the company and explain why they chose to name that person. The "heroes" of an organization can act as role models for current employees IF they understand why those folks are considered heroes.
- Listen to the stories, myths, and rumors that are told by employees. What are the core messages that they are attempting to relate? What are the "inside jokes" at your company?
- Are there rituals and ceremonies that are sacred to employees? What are they, and when do they occur? Who is involved in carrying them out?

Are there employees who are not involved in them and, if so, why not? How do those employees feel who are not included?

- Who are the "storytellers," "gossipers," "whisperers," "priests/priestesses," and "spies" in your organization? How might you tap into these characters as you build coalitions, implement changes, and pursue new goals?

Remember, using these questions and observations can help managers be more successful in all their management roles. And, importantly, they can help managers know how best to shape a culture for all the planned changes that will occur, as well as to understand why and how employees will react during times of uncertainty.

Concluding Thoughts

You've now learned three ways to "see" organizations from different perspectives. Which lens managers use depends on their personal preference (some managers naturally are attracted to one more than the others), the situation that presents itself, and the problems or challenges they face. Moreover, *effective* managers can use all of the approaches for making decisions, leading change, motivating employees, allocating scarce resources, and building relationships across multiple boundaries. The key is knowing if and when design, politics, or culture is the more important consideration in the decision or which presents the largest barrier to change in the moment.

Becoming a manager is not easy. It requires some very basic understanding of the organization you serve, the people who count on you to lead them, and the competency and accountability for the job you hold. But being a manager is an important job in every organization. Hopefully, you will find it is personally rewarding as well!

What's Next?

In addition to the managerial roles of strategic designer, politician, and cultural visionary, there are several roles that managers play and which you must master to be an effective manager. The first of these—"Leader"—is generally considered to be one of the most important, and we will look at several aspects of "Manager as Leader" in the next three chapters.

Additional Reading, Resources, and Activities

In order to get the most out of what you've already read and to practice putting the strategic design, political, and cultural concepts in action, the following are some additional helpful resources and activities.

- Although it has already been cited in this chapter, the beginning chapters in the book by Ancona et al. are excellent to get a more in-depth understanding of all three lenses (Ancona, D., Kochan, T., Maureen, S., Van Maanen, J., & Westney, E. (1996, 1999, 2005). *Managing for the future: Organizational behavior and processes* (1–3 eds.). South-Western College Publishing.).

- Look at an organization chart of a larger organization (more than 200 employees). How is the company organized—by function, product, customer, or geography? What might be a downside for the particular organization being structured that way? What formal linking mechanisms do you see on the chart? If there are no formal ones, where might some informal ones be needed?

- Watch the movie, "Twelve Angry Men," starring Henry Fonda. Describe some clear evidence of "schema" differences brought to the jury room. What role did power and influence play for each of the jurors? What influence techniques did the architect use to persuade each juror to reexamine his initial verdict? Who used power and influence poorly?

- Walk around an organization that you are very familiar with (your place of work, your school, your church) and look for artifacts that speak to the values, mission, meaning, and life of that organization. What do they tell you about "how things are done" there? Interview a manager and an employee who work there. Ask them to tell you a story or describe a hero that captures the essence of the culture for them. What specific aspect of the culture does the story or hero represent?

- Watch the 2006 movie, "Outsourced." Identify some of the culture "clashes" that occur between Todd, the American manager, and the Indian employees in terms of history, values and beliefs, symbols, rituals, and ceremonies. The 1986 movie, "Gung Ho!" starring Michael Keaton, also presents some good examples of culture clash between a unionized manufacturing plant and its new Asian owners. Either one of these films will make clear the difficulties of trying to merge or change organizational cultures.

Manager as Leader: Emotional Intelligence and Competency

2

The best of all rulers is but a shadowy presence to his subjects.

> *Next comes the ruler they love and praise;*
>
> *Next comes one they fear;*
>
> *Next comes one with whom they take liberties . . .*
>
> *Hesitant, the best does not utter words lightly.*
>
> *When his task is accomplished and his work done*
>
> *The people all say, "It happened to us naturally."*

> *—Excerpted from the Tao Te Ching,*
> *by Lao Tzu, ancient Chinese philosopher and writer*

What does it mean to be a leader?

There are many definitions of leadership, and yet most people can't really put their finger on any one specific trait or behavior that definitively says, "That's it!" But aren't we usually able to recognize a leader when we see one? As Reid Gervais writes,

> *What it means to be a leader, in our modern context, is defined in a broader sense more than any other time in history. Leadership takes on a form that is represented as an integrated model of behavior and perspective that involves every thought, word, and action in a person's life. The premise of leadership stems from the willingness and commitment to assume responsibility. This responsibility is not restricted to a specific event or program but in a more general way, a way of demonstrating a person's ability to display trust, respect, tolerance, and compassion in such a manner that another person will deem it something of value and purpose to follow, and take direction from.*

> *—Excerpted from "Destiny by Your Own Hand," by Reid Gervais.*

In an organization, managers who demonstrate leadership capabilities are, first and foremost, in tune with their own feelings and emotions and are able to control them, even when publically challenged on their decisions. Though they may feel anger when someone disagrees with them, they don't show it on their faces or in their body language. They are also able to read others' feelings and emotions so that they are able to communicate with empathy and understanding. For these managers not only can see the fear in an employee's eyes when faced with a new task, they are able to explain how they, too, felt some trepidation the first time they did the task. Finally, they are able to seek out and manage complex relationships with others by adapting their communication style. They can recognize when an employee isn't learning how to do something and change their language or approach in how they explain it. In short, effective leaders are able to demonstrate competence in building relationships, and this begins by understanding the extent to which they possess *emotional intelligence.*

What Are Emotionally Intelligent Leaders?

The idea that we have multiple intelligences, rather than just one (like IQ), was first introduced by Howard Gardner in his book, *Frames of Mind: The Theory of Multiple Intelligences.*[1] Since 1999, Gardner has identified eight intelligences in all: linguistic, logical-mathematical, musical, spatial, bodily/kinesthetic, interpersonal, intrapersonal, and naturalistic.[2] Among these you will note *interpersonal intelligence* (the capacity to understand the intentions, motivations, and desires of other people) and *intrapersonal intelligence* (the capacity to understand oneself, to appreciate one's feelings, fears, and motivations). These form the basis of the notion that we all have an "emotional intelligence quotient" or "EQ."

In 1995 Daniel Goleman wrote the bestseller, *Emotional Intelligence.*[3] In it, he describes emotional intelligence as having both "self" and "other" dimensions (see Figure 1)—in essence, the competence to be aware of our own and others' emotions, as well as to regulate our own emotions and manage relationships with others. As leaders, having a high "EQ" is crucial because, without the ability to regulate our own emotions and pick up on the emotions

---

[1] Gardner, H. (1983). *Frames of mind: The theory of multiple intelligences.* New York: Basic Books.

[2] Gardner, H. (1999). *Intelligence reframed: Multiple intelligences for the 21st century.* New York: Basic Books.

[3] Goleman, D. (1995). *Emotional intelligence.* New York: Bantam Books.

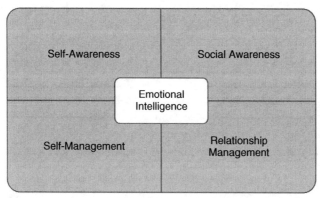

Figure 1 Goleman's (1995) Emotional Intelligence Model
....
Source: Dale J. Dwyer

of others, we will not be able to develop meaningful relationships with our employees, nor will we be seen as credible and trustworthy.

Interestingly, unlike a standard "IQ" or intelligence quotient, Goleman believes that "EQ" or emotional quotient is not comprised of innate talents, but rather learned capabilities that must be worked on and that can be developed to achieve better relationships. If Goleman is correct, as leaders we all need to work on developing and improving our emotional intelligence competency.

Goleman's model is comprised of two dimensions: *awareness* of emotions and *management* of emotions, and these are focused either on the *self* or on *others*. One of the hallmarks of high emotional intelligence is self-awareness. *Self-awareness* is a deep understanding of what makes us tick. It allows us to recognize what angers us, makes us happy, attracts our interest, or bores us. It also means that we can appraise ourselves, faults and all, with great honesty and clarity.

Here are some specific characteristics that a self-aware leader demonstrates:

- They are able to recognize which emotions they feel and why.
- They realize the links between those emotions and their behaviors.
- They know their strengths and limitations.
- They are able to learn from experience, remaining open to feedback, new perspectives, and personal development.
- They present themselves with confidence, poise, and assurance.
- They can voice unpopular views, but are decisive despite uncertainty and external pressure.

A second aspect to an emotionally intelligent leader is the recognition that they must manage their own emotions. *Self-management* entails being able to

- Manage impulsive feelings and distressing emotions,
- Think clearly and stay focused under pressure,
- Stay composed and positive, even in trying situations,
- Handle multiple demands and rapid change,
- Adapt their responses to fit changing circumstances,
- Hold themselves accountable for meeting their objectives,
- Keep promises they make,
- Operate from a position of hope rather than of fear,
- Mobilize others through unusual, enterprising efforts,
- Entertain multiple solutions to problems,
- Seek out different perspectives from a variety of sources, and
- Persist in pursuing goals despite setbacks.

One of the more crucial competencies for the emotionally intelligent leader is to develop *social awareness* of others' feelings and perspectives. Examples of these characteristics include

- Showing empathy and sensitivity,
- Being attentive to emotional cues and sensing what others need in the moment,
- Listening "underneath" the words that are said to correctly understand meaning,
- Reading situations and power relationships correctly,
- Acknowledging people's strengths and accomplishments,
- Giving timely coaching, and offering assignments that challenge and grow a person's skills,
- Respecting and relating well to people with diverse worldviews, and
- Challenging bias and intolerance.

Finally, to become more emotionally intelligent requires us to be able to influence others, communicate clearly, resolve conflicts without apportioning blame, and manage relationships. Leaders skilled at *relationship management* are able to

- Build consensus and support,
- Deal with difficult issues in a straightforward manner,
- Bring disagreements into the open and de-escalate tension,

- Orchestrate win-win solutions to conflicts,
- Guide the performance of others while holding them accountable,
- Arouse enthusiasm for a shared vision,
- Recognize the need for change and remove barriers to it,
- Challenge the status quo,
- Collaborate with others,
- Build rapport and bonds that are mutually beneficial, and
- Share credit for "wins" and accomplishments of their colleagues and teams.

Becoming an Emotionally Intelligent Leader

The goal, of course, is to become proficient and competent at all four aspects of emotional intelligence. It is likely, though, that at least most of us fall a bit short in one or more of them. In order to see where you might fall in each of these areas, you might consider taking one of the assessments available online, some of which are free.[4]

Why do many of us have difficulty becoming more emotionally competent?

Part of the reason may be that we don't try very hard. In *The Fifth Discipline*, Peter M. Senge quotes an article called "Advanced Maturity," written by Bill O'Brien, and it is worth reproducing here:

> *Whatever the reasons, we do not pursue emotional development with the same intensity with which we pursue physical and intellectual development. This is all the more unfortunate, because full emotional development offers the greatest degree of leverage in attaining our full potential.*[5]

Another reason is that we are continually fighting against our ancestral brains. Dr. Paul D. MacLean, a prominent brain researcher, developed a model of brain structure that he calls the "triune brain" (Figure 2). In other words, humans have not one brain, but three interconnected biological computers, each having "its own special intelligence, its own subjectivity, its own sense

---

[4] As an example, http://globalleadershipfoundation.com/geit/eitest.html, The Global Emotional Intelligence Test uses 40 questions that are derived from the Global *EI Capability Assessment* instrument, which contains 158 items. These are based on Goleman's four quadrant Emotional Intelligence Competency Model (2002). Short EI quizzes such as the GEIT are meant to be fun, and to give you pointers about EI areas where you are doing well and areas that you may need to focus on for development.

[5] Senge, P. (2006). *The fifth discipline: The art and practice of the learning organization.* New York: Doubleday, p. 133.

of time and space, its own memory, motor, and other functions."[6] Each of the three brains corresponds to a major evolutionary development, categorized as follows: the reptilian brain or cerebellum (survival functions), the old mammalian brain or limbic system (emotional functions), and the new mammalian brain or neocortex (reasoning functions).

Human physiology has evolved over millions of years. From the time primordial sea creatures crawled onto land, the adaptation of their physical and mental abilities began. In human brains, the most ancient and smallest of the three brains evolved because of a need to survive under adverse conditions. This small brain is around 200 million years old and is referred to as the *reptilian brain*. Much of human behavior can be described in reptilian terms, especially those involving aggression and territoriality. It primarily regulates the "fight or flight" response, breathing, heart rate, and other autonomic functions.

The old mammalian brain, or the *limbic system*, is sandwiched between the reptilian brain and the new mammalian brain or neocortex. This brain evolved about 60 million years ago, over 100+ million years after the original reptilian brain. It is far more sensitive and sophisticated than the reptilian brain. The limbic system is concerned with the emotions, and it plays a different, but nevertheless major, role in aggression and fear. It is largely responsible for the resetting of various bodily systems during our emotional reactions. The limbic system also is thought to be the origin of altruistic, as well as sexual, behaviors.

The newest brain, the *neocortex* or new mammalian brain, only developed a few million years ago. In humans, the neocortex is also the largest of the three brains, accounting for about five-sixths of the entire human brain. It is responsible for higher-order thinking skills, reason, linguistic expression, and verbal memory. The job of the neocortex is to detect patterns and interpret the meanings of situations. In essence, it is this large, higher-order thinking part of our brain that distinguishes humans from other species.

Humans rely heavily on the neocortex to *interpret* events. Let's say that it is almost dusk, and you are walking in the woods. You notice a long, slender, black object right in front of you on the path. You may initially have a "flight" response (from the reptilian part of your brain), followed by a surge of adrenaline (from the limbic system), because you think it is a snake. But, after using our neocortex that has "stored" the images of both a snake and a tree branch, you reasonably interpret the object to be a tree branch!

---

[6] MacLean, P. D. (1993). Evolution of three mentalities. In J. B. Ashbrook (Ed.), *Brain, culture, and the human spirit: Essays from an emergent evolutionary perspective* (p. 24). Lanham, MD: University Press of America.

Figure 2 The Triune Brain and Its Functions

© Kendall Hunt Publishing Company

Reptilian Brain (Cerebellum)	Old Mammalian Brain (Limbic System)	New Mammalian Brain (Neocortex)
• "Fight" or "Flight" • Automatic Thoughts	• Emotions • Memories • Sexual Response	• Language • Rational Thought • Imagination

The Role of Automatic Thoughts

In many instances, emotional responses are directly preceded by automatic thoughts, that is, those thoughts that have developed over time based on previous experiences, conditioning, and so on. They often arise from specific internal needs—such as the need for approval or control—and from unresolved developmental conflicts from our childhood. For example, if we speak with someone and they start smiling, we might interpret that smile in one of two ways: either that they are laughing at us or that they could be pleased at something we said. If we have a history of being teased, and we let automatic thought prevail, we may interpret the smile as negative and believe the person is making fun of us. Our reaction, then, would be based on our negative perception and interpretation of the other person's behavior (their smile).

Automatic thoughts remain hidden beneath the surface for most people. They don't realize they are having them. When automatic thoughts control our emotional responses to people, problems, and events, we ignore evidence that contradicts the automatic thought. It is when we allow ourselves to be controlled by our survival or emotional brains—without feedback from the neocortex—that we run into problems. Unless we train ourselves to look for these thoughts, we will probably be unaware of them. Getting a handle on our emotions is a matter of gaining conscious control over those thoughts that occur automatically. Emotional control is essentially a matter of detaching ourselves from our negative emotions that are brought on by self-defeating automatic thoughts. Without developing an ability to become aware of and control emotions, leaders will always be challenged by their own behavior and, ultimately, gaining the trust of others. In reality, this ability requires continual practice for most people.

Practices to Develop Emotional Control

As many of us have discovered to our detriment, an inability to control one's emotions or to be aware of others' emotional cues is a potentially career-ending challenge. This inability is our old reptilian brains or our limbic systems taking over our reasoning brain. A number of researchers, including Daniel Goleman, have argued that leaders fail most often because of their inability to manage their emotions and moods, as well as their inability to empathize and get along with others.[7] In other words, emotional intelligence is more predictive of success in relating to others (e.g., bosses, peers, direct reports, customers) than many other personality or behavioral predictors.

To that end, here is one way to get a handle on your own automatic thoughts.

- *Discover the validity of "automatic thoughts"* by keeping a record for 2 weeks. Write down what event or situation prompted the thought, your thoughts immediately following, the emotion you felt about it, and what you actually did (behavior). You could use a form that looks something like this:

Event	Emotions	Automatic Thoughts	Logical Comebacks

The *event* is a factual description with no emotions attached. For example, you might say, "Clothes shopping with my sister," rather than "Sister acting like she knows everything I should buy on a shopping trip."

---

[7] Goleman, D. (1995). *Emotional intelligence.* New York: Bantam Books.

The latter statement contains your interpretation of the event, which would be more properly listed in the "automatic thoughts" column.

Your *emotions* describe how you feel about the event. Be sure not to confuse feelings with thoughts. Rather than saying, "I feel as if my sister thinks I'm stupid" (which is actually a belief), describe how you feel about your sister thinking you're stupid. Are you feeling angry? Do you feel hurt? Are you indignant? Do you feel vulnerable?

Your *automatic thoughts* are the beliefs attached to and the meanings you have assigned to events. What did you say to yourself in response to the event? What went through your mind? For example, an automatic thought associated with the event, "shopping with my sister," might be "My sister thinks I have no judgment in clothes." It is important to pinpoint the automatic thought that is causing your feelings of anger, hurt, or vulnerability.

Beck and his colleagues[8] recommend monitoring your thoughts and identifying how they have become distorted so that you can choose the most appropriate response. See if you recognize any of your distorted and automatic thoughts here:

- *Mental filtering*: Focusing on the negative details and magnifying them, while filtering out all positive aspects of a situation. Think about a performance situation in which you have focused on all the things you are doing "wrong," rather than those things you are doing "right."
- *Dichotomous thinking*: Things are either/or, black/white, good/bad, perfect or a complete failure. There is no "gray" area, no middle ground.
- *Mind reading*: Can you suddenly read minds and know exactly what people are thinking, especially with regard to you? Unfortunately, this generally results in even more distorted and dichotomous thinking.
- *Catastrophic exaggeration*: You believe the worst-case scenario is going to occur (i.e., think Chicken Little's "the sky is falling").
- *Blaming others*: This is a classic example of holding other people solely responsible for your own situation, particularly if the outcomes are not favorable or positive to you.
- *Externally controlled*: Feeling completely at the mercy of external forces, you may believe that you will never be able to regain control. This often results in paranoia that causes you to suspect others of nefarious behavior.

---

[8] Beck, A. T., Kovacs, M., & Weissman, A. (1979). Assessment of suicidal intention: The Scale for Suicide Ideation. *Journal of Consulting and Clinical Psychology*, 47(2), 343–352.

To determine whether a belief is completely accurate ask yourself, "What evidence do I have to support the belief?" and "What evidence do I have that refutes it?" These questions are useful in identifying thoughts that are biased in that they do not consider all available information. Beliefs like, "I've made a complete fool of myself" and "No one likes me" are almost always distorted.

Draw a line down the middle of a piece of paper and put the data supporting the automatic thought on the left side and the data that refute it on the right side. If you have any data whatsoever on the right side (usually there will be at least some), then the automatic thought is necessarily biased or missing data.

Once you have determined the legitimacy or illegitimacy of your automatic thoughts you will need to decide how to change your reaction to them. One way to do this is to decide on *logical comebacks* that provide you another response to the event, rather than allowing the automatic ones to continue unrestrained. In other words, what would be a more realistic way of thinking? What modifications to the belief would make it more balanced? Obviously you are looking for an emotionally competent response in your comeback.

In the above example, it is apparent that the automatic thought, "My sister thinks I'm stupid" or "My sister thinks I have no judgment in clothes" was probably distorted at the very least. A much more realistic interpretation might be something like, "The fact that my sister gives me advice on which clothes to buy tells me she cares about my appearance. I generally DO look good in the clothes she's recommended in the past."

It is important to capitalize on every opportunity to counter automatic negative thoughts. In time, if you keep at it, you will notice that a reasonable examination of automatic thoughts will become second nature—maybe even automatic!

Concluding Thoughts

To begin the process of improving your emotional intelligence—or any leadership behavior for that matter—the emotional centers need repetition and practice. Improving emotional intelligence is akin to changing old habits, by replacing the old behaviors with new ones. The more often you practice becoming aware of your own emotions, picking up emotional cues from others, regulating and managing your emotions, and being attentive to the relationships with your direct reports, peers, and bosses, the more these behaviors will become second nature and the more competent you will be perceived by those around you.

Besides emotional competence, there are other aspects of leadership that all of us can develop more fully. In the next chapter, we look at a second leadership skill that all influential leaders need to develop: charisma.

Additional Reading, Resources, and Activities

In order to get the most out of what you've already read and to begin to develop your own emotional competence, the following are some additional helpful resources and activities.

- The movie, "Horrible Bosses," starring Kevin Spacey, is a great example of a bullying boss with very little emotional intelligence. As you watch it, think about where he "misses" picking up on social cues, doesn't control his own emotional responses to his employees, and generally has poor relationships with everyone he meets.

- Take one of the Emotional Competence Inventories that are free online, such as the Global Emotional Intelligence Test mentioned earlier. See where you need to concentrate your "automatic thought" analysis and where you might develop alternative responses in the areas you are the most challenged. http://globalleadershipfoundation.com/geit/eitest.html

- In order to develop more empathy, try writing a timeline of your own major life events, positive or negative, and sharing your "story" with another person. The person should just listen without commentary for five minutes and then ask you questions. Switch places and listen to the other person's story. What did you learn about each other that you never knew before? How many experiences did each of you have that were commonly shared? Did you have any that were completely different? How might shared experiences help you develop more empathy for others?

Manager as Leader: Charisma and Style

3

How can you have charisma? Be more concerned about making others feel good about themselves than you are making them feel good about you."

—Dan Reiland, author

Of course, all the competence in the world will not necessarily make you an effective leader unless you can inspire and motivate your direct reports to engage with you in your efforts. In this, another aspect of leadership is needed: *charisma.*

Much has been written about the notion of charisma and its role in leadership. But it is so much more than just charm and attraction. As Marianne Williamson, internationally acclaimed author and speaker, writes, "We need less posturing and more genuine charisma. Charisma was originally a religious term, meaning 'of the spirit' or 'inspired.' It's about letting God's light shine through us. It's about a sparkle in people that money can't buy. It's an invisible energy with visible effects ...."[1]

Although charisma's origins were about having a divine gift, charisma today is viewed more as personal attributes or a style, particularly as it applies to leadership. In organizations, charismatic leadership depends on leaders and followers sharing ideological values and is determined by how the leader uses power—power that is based on emotion and ideology. Thus, it doesn't depend on or use rewards, coercion, or expertise to influence followers. Rather, a leader who possesses charisma is highly influential because of personal characteristics and behaviors that create a feeling of moral unity among followers.[2] In essence, "the invisible energy with visible effects."

---

[1] Williamson, M. (2006). *The Gift of Change: Spiritual Guidance for Living Your Best Life.* Harper Collins Publishers.

[2] Keyes, C. F. (2002). Weber and anthropology. *Annual Review of Anthropology,* 31: 233–255.

How Charismatic Leaders Emerge

It is worth noting that many people believe that one either has or does not have charisma; that is, it cannot be learned. But I disagree. I believe that charisma gets its power from the extent to which a person can demonstrate, verbally and non-verbally, the characteristics of optimism, confidence, approachability, and authenticity of convictions. But we must also remember that "the charismatic leader is always the creation of his followers. That is, charismatic authority is rooted in the belief system of the followers, rather than in some transcendental characteristic of the leader."[3] As such, the question for managers is more about conveying the characteristics well enough so that followers perceive the leader to be positive, authentic, and inspiring.

The birth of a charismatic leader is most likely to occur in a climate of uncertainty and unpredictability. An individual presents himself in a time of need and initially inspires a small group of believers. Eventually all those predisposed to the coming of a new order will respond to the leader's voicing common grievances by giving him their support.[4]

As has already been mentioned in our discussion of the Cultural lens, each organizational culture has a body of myth that explains the past, present, as well as the future. It gives a people an identity, something in common that ties them together. When a leader is able to associate himself and his message with this communal myth, he validates his authority. The strategy for achieving this association with myth includes rhetoric employed in speeches, allusions to myth and history, the use of gesture and movement, the employment of ritual and ceremony, and the manner of dealing with doubt and crisis.

Consider the rise of Adolph Hitler who associated his political party with an historical, almost mythical, view of German culture that inspired followers. He derived his charismatic power from this myth and helped perpetuate it by using symbols, ceremony, speeches, and propaganda. Rev. Dr. Martin Luther King, Jr. also became the center figure in the pursuit of civil rights, primarily because he was passionate, well-spoken, and respected.

Despite the notion that one either has "it" or not, research has shown that people can be taught to be more charismatic with training in communication style and by providing improvement feedback to them.[5] So, let's look at some

---

[3] Fagen, R.R. (1965). Charismatic authority and the leadership of Fidel Castro. *Western Political Quarterly*, 18, 275.

[4] Miner, A.R. and Willner, D. (1965). "The Rise and Role of Charismatic Leaders." *American Academy of Political and Social Science Annals*, 358, 77–88.

[5] Antonakis, J., Fenley, M., and Liechti, S. (2011). Can charisma be taught? Tests of two interventions. *Academy of Management Learning & Education*, 10, 3, 374–396.

ways to convey charisma so you will be able to incorporate them into your own leadership development.

Conveying Charisma

Leaders are attributed charisma because they can communicate in vivid and emotional ways that paint an attainable vision for their followers. It is not only *what* leaders say, but also *how* they say it. Verbal communication and speechmaking has taught us that the "medium is the message"[6] and, therefore, people have a tendency to interpret the content of a leader's communication by how and when it is delivered.

Charismatic leaders have a strong sense of mission, as well as an uncompromising belief both in the movement and in themselves as the chosen person to lead the movement. As a whole these leaders seem to show unusual powers of vision and communication. They are able to quickly grasp a situation, even if it is new to them, and just as quickly formulate a response that is consistent with their movement. Stubborn self-confidence, limitless faith in their ability to influence change, and a righteous sense of purpose seem to surround these inspirational leaders.

Consider some of the historical figures who are considered to epitomize a charismatic leader: Dr. Martin Luther King, Jr., Adolph Hitler, Winston Churchill, John F. Kennedy, Ronald Reagan, Cesar Chavez, Napoleon Bonaparte, Maria Eva Duarte Perón, Mahatma Gandhi, Nelson Mandela, and countless others. Not all of these people had a positive message, but all of them were able to create an emotional connection with their followers through using very specific rhetorical devices and messages that resonated with their specific followers. All of the following devices can be taught and learned by any leader who seeks to create an emotional connection with her followers:

- *Metaphors*: Generally, a metaphor is a figure of speech that uses a word or phrase to suggest a likeness or analogy with another object or idea. A cultural metaphor is any activity or phenomenon with which most members of a given culture identify cognitively or emotionally. One example might be "time is money." Others might use sports metaphors to refer to achieving a goal ("she hit a homerun with that sale") or motivating employees (referring to managers as "coaches"). All organizations develop an inside language and jargon that is understood by their members, but metaphors are particularly useful for leaders, because they can

---

[6] McLuhan, M. (1964). *Understanding Media: The Extensions of Man*. New York: McGraw-Hill.

be used to connect employees to the culture the leaders wish to establish, teach, and reinforce.

- *Anecdotes, Parables and Stories*: In essence, all three of these are stories told to teach the listener something. Anecdotes are generally quick mini-stories that are told to make one point. Parables use human characters that give some instruction to the listener in how to behave or teach some moral lesson. Stories are usually longer and have more vivid detail than anecdotes. All of them, however, are used to focus the attention of the audience, challenge a commonly held belief or attitude and, of course, to make a point in a way that everyone can understand and remember. Leaders can use stories that relate to changes that may be coming, describe people who are the heroes (or the villains) of the company, or reference historical achievements of their organizations that have formed the basis for the current values and mission. The stories leaders tell can help shape the culture, too, not just reinforce it. In other words, change the stories you tell, and people will begin to change how they think and behave. As Howard Gardner wrote, "Stories are the single most powerful tool in a leader's toolkit."[7]
- *Contrasts and Similarities*: Sometimes it is difficult for employees to make distinctions between appropriate behaviors and ethical choices, or even which thorny problem to focus on. When a leader uses a contrast (e.g., pointing out the poor outcomes of treating customers as a nuisance vs. choosing a successful and ethical approach to serving customers), he focuses employees on the desired message and away from the undesirable one. In the same way, relating a difficult decision about to be faced by employees can be made less scary if the leader can point out a similar decision employees have already experienced in the past.
- *Rhetorical Questions*: Leaders may ask rhetorical questions to make a point, to build anticipation, or to create a dramatic effect. Although there is no expected answer to a rhetorical question, asking employees, "Can our customers expect us to do better?" "Can we expect ourselves to do better?" may not elicit an actual answer, but it will challenge, engage, and motivate employees to focus on improvement.

In addition to rhetorical devices, the content itself should carry the leader's convictions about the value of the vision, the worth of the change, or the high expectations for their followers. By expressing confidence in their followers to be able to achieve lofty goals, as well as to provide moral support

---

[7] Gardner, H.E. (1998). The intelligence of leaders. *International Journal of Leadership in Education*, 1, 2, pp. 203–06.

as they attempt them, charismatic leaders create an almost euphoric, positive feeling in their followers. Charismatic leaders are also masters at conveying their passion and emotions through non-verbal means. How they move, the tone and variety in their voice, and their facial expressions make their message more meaningful and memorable for their employees.

Remember that each of these devices and approaches can be taught and learned. Ronald Riggio, Ph.D., a professor of organizational psychology at Claremont McKenna College, has spent much of his career studying how to develop a more charismatic personality. In the following section we will look at several ways he has found to be useful so that you can begin to develop your own style.

Developing Charisma

Becoming more charismatic has to be learned through preparation and practice. But first, we have to be able to identify some specific behaviors so that we can adapt them for ourselves. One way to learn what charismatic people do is to watch them speak in public and observe how their listeners react. For example, does the audience perk up and pay attention, or are they playing with their phones? Are the facial expressions on the audience members happy or sad, excited or bored? And, most importantly, does the leader express confidence, optimism, and hope for the audience in her speech? If so, that leader is probably considered to be charismatic by her followers.

You can also watch film clips of speeches by great motivational speakers, such as Martin Luther King, Jr., or the "Most Popular Talks of All Time" (Ted talks)[8], paying attention to the rhetorical devices they use, their facial expressions, the variety of tone, pitch, and volume in their voices, and how passionately they convey their messages. Exactly emulating these great speakers is not the goal; rather, trying out some of their techniques will help you discover what is comfortable and effective for you. To be clear, charismatic leaders have to be perceived to be authentically themselves. But practicing some tried-and-true rhetorical devices will allow you to incorporate more of them into your own leadership communication style.

You might also try filming yourself as you speak, which will allow you to realize how you are coming across to others, i.e., whether you're mumbling, fidgeting, lacking passion, etc.

Remember that being charismatic, along with your perceived competence, allows you to inspire others and motivate them to do the hard work that is necessary in bringing about change in organizations.

---

[8] https://www.ted.com/playlists/171/the_most_popular_talks_of_all

In addition to the rhetorical devices mentioned earlier, Riggio suggests several other ways to become more charismatic:[9]

- **Practice showing your emotions, not hiding them**. Our faces are the windows to understand and share important information about what we are feeling, perceiving or desiring. On the other hand, sometimes we do not want to share our emotions, particularly if we are frustrated or angry, and so it is just as important to practice controlling our emotions. Appearing "calm, cool, and collected" in a trying situation is attractive to most people and makes them want to be like you.
- **Focus on being present and really listening to others.** This is another key skill related to charisma. When you are truly present and focus on what another person is saying, rather than thinking about what you want to say in return, you demonstrate care and concern. You also tend to learn things you may not have expected to learn!
- **Develop an ability to read others' emotions.** As we saw in the previous chapter, emotional intelligence is part becoming aware and controlling your own emotions, and part reading others' emotions and learning the appropriate responses. This holds true in one-on-one conversations, in group settings, and in your own public addresses to your department or organization. Reading the "temperature" of the room is one of the ways charismatic leaders learn what to highlight or what to avoid in their communication with others.
- **Use words that resonate with your audience.** Think about how advertisements and TV commercials appeal to their audience to buy something. You would not likely hear a spokesperson for a car talk about the mechanical parts. Rather, the advertising appeal is focused on the audience's experience as they drive the car, like the feel of the soft leather or the rich sounds of the high-end radio. It is a good lesson for charismatic leaders to learn: use concrete, sensory language that speaks to their hearts, not to their brains.

BEWARE! The Two sides of Charismatic Leadership

While it is a valuable skill to develop, becoming more charismatic has both a "light" and a "dark" side. Developing into an ethical charismatic and competent leader requires several things of you. Specifically, ethical charismatic leaders

---

[9] Riggio, R.E. (1987). *The charisma quotient*. New York: Dodd, Mead Publishers.

- use their vision and influence to serve others,
- demonstrate resilience in the face of opposition,
- partner with others to accomplish greater things than they ever could alone,
- develop their followers' capabilities to continue the movement and strive toward the vision, and
- recognize when new approaches, new leadership, or a new vision is needed.

Rev. Dr. Martin Luther King, Jr. typifies all of these characteristics. When King arose as the primary leader of the bus boycott in Montgomery, Alabama, he did so as a reluctant leader, chosen by the citizens of Montgomery, because he was relatively young, was too new in town to have made enemies, and was generally respected as clergy.

King understood the power of television to nationalize and internationalize the struggle for civil rights, and his well-publicized tactics of active nonviolence (e.g., sit-ins, protest marches) aroused the devoted allegiance of many African-Americans and liberal whites in all parts of the country, as well as support from the administrations of Presidents Kennedy and Lyndon B. Johnson. He formed the Southern Christian Leadership Conference (SCLC) so that he could widen the vision, as well as gain participation, nationally.

Joining with other clergy and political leaders, King organized the historic March on Washington in 1963 to demand equal justice for all citizens under the law. He next sought to widen his base by forming a coalition of the poor of all races that would address itself to economic problems such as poverty and unemployment. It was a version of populism—seeking to enroll janitors, hospital workers, seasonal laborers, and the destitute, along with student militants and pacifist intellectuals.

During the time he was prominent as a Civil Rights leader, his home was bombed, his family threatened, he was imprisoned several times, and his own personal safety was constantly in question. Although he was assassinated just months before his 40th birthday, he remains one of the most inspiring leaders of the 20th century who, with dogged determination and resilience, continued to develop and motivate followers toward his vision of justice and the beloved community.

On the other hand, we can identify unethical charismatic leaders who, in contrast with leaders like King,

- focus on their own personal goals, not for those that benefit others,
- concentrate on increasing their power and control over followers,
- censure opposing views, including the free press,

- are narcissistic and believe that they are infallible, and
- articulate a message that incites their followers, leading them to their own destruction or to the annihilation of others

As an example of an unethical, but nevertheless charismatic, leader, Adolph Hitler rose to power after the humiliating defeat of Germany in World War I. From the first he set out to create a mass movement, whose mystique and power would be sufficient to bind its members in loyalty to him. He engaged in unrelenting propaganda through the Nazi party newspaper and through meetings whose audiences soon grew from a handful to thousands.

With his charismatic personality and dynamic leadership, he also attracted a devoted cadre of Nazi leaders. He became their leader with almost unlimited powers and very pro-Aryan ideas, particularly anti-Semitism.

Once in power, Hitler established an absolute dictatorship. As an example, he deliberately created offices with overlapping authority, thus effectively preventing any one office or person from ever becoming sufficiently strong to challenge his own absolute authority. Hitler combined opportunism and clever timing. He showed astonishing skill in judging the mood of the democratic leaders in Western Europe and exploiting their weaknesses—in spite of the fact that he scarcely set foot outside his homeland. By far, though, his main focus was on the extermination of the Jews, although Catholics, Poles, homosexuals, Gypsies, and the handicapped were also targeted. By virtue of his censure of the free press, his dynamic and charismatic personality, and the repetitive message that Germans were superior to all others, he managed to convince a nation that he was their savior. Ultimately realizing he would not prevail, he took his own life and that of his long-time mistress and recent wife, Eva Braun, in a secluded bunker in April 1945 as World War II finally wound down, finally ending in September of that year.

Concluding Thoughts

Managers who demonstrate leadership competency and who are able to motivate and inspire others to follow them toward a new vision for their organizations are rare. Part of the reason has to do with some underlying needs that tend to undermine the trustworthiness and credibility of even the most well-intentioned leader/manager. In the next chapter we examine two of the most important needs that underlie many of the challenges that undermine trustworthiness and credibility and that often derail managerial careers: Need for Control and Need for Approval.

Additional Reading, Resources, and Activities

In order to get the most out of what you've already read and to see Charismatic Leaders in action, the following are some additional helpful resources and activities.

- Watch video biographies about the lives of Rev. Dr. Martin Luther King, Jr. and Adolph Hitler.

  - What challenges did these charismatic leaders face?

  - What are the similarities and differences between King and Hitler in terms of leadership traits, behaviors, and vision?

  - Thinking about both leaders (and any other charismatic leaders you've known), why do you think people follow charismatic leaders?

- Read MLK's "Letter from a Birmingham Jail." In this letter, where do you see the characteristics of an ethical Charismatic Leader discussed in this chapter? What do you think King was trying to accomplish with this letter?

- Interview a manager to see if he or she possesses some of the characteristics of a Charismatic Leader. If the manager you interview is one for whom you work, do you think he or she is charismatic? Why or why not?

Manager as Leader: When Needs for Control and Approval Undermine Leadership

> *The best years of your life are the ones in which you decide your problems are your own. You don't blame them on your mother, the ecology, or the President. You realize that you control your own destiny.*
>
> —*Albert Ellis, Clinical Psychologist and founder of Rational Emotive Behavioral Therapy*

We have talked about the competency and charisma necessary to be a successful and effective leader. There are, however, some deep-seated needs that we all have that can hijack our leadership behaviors to a point that threatens our credibility and trustworthiness IF they get too extreme. These two needs are need for control and need for approval. It is worth some discussion here, because without understanding these needs, you may be undermining all the good work you have attempted as you develop your emotional competence and charisma.

Need for Control

Control is a fundamental human and animal need; first and foremost, it is a survival tool that is used to avoid being taken advantage of by others. We likely get it from our earliest prehistoric ancestors. It is a response to go on the offensive and to take a position of strength in our environment. However, an overly controlling response occurs when relinquishing control becomes so distressing that it results in an obsession with maintaining that control—a type of obsessive-compulsive personality trait. This can result in the inability to accept new courses of action, even when it is in our best interests to do so. It also can lead to feeling overly concerned for the welfare of others to the point that they may feel impotent in dealing with their own situations and behaviors. People who are overly controlling tend to squash others' creativity, tread on individual rights and responsibilities, and generally try to create a culture of automatons. Moreover, they often lose perspective on situations.

There is an old story told by philosopher and psychologist, William James,[1] of a man who slid down a cliff on a very dark night. Obviously scared, he caught hold of a branch that stopped his fall; for hours he remained clinging to the branch, trying desperately to hold on for dear life. Gradually, he felt the strength go out of his arms, and he finally realized that his muscles just couldn't hold on any longer. With a despairing farewell to life, he let go ... and dropped onto a ledge that was just six inches below him! So much of his agony could have been spared if he could have seen his situation in the proper perspective and stopped struggling to maintain control.

Many people adopt a controlling approach *because* of their past experiences with letting go of control. If they believe that they were taken advantage of in the past, they don't want that to happen again. Going to the extreme, they make sure that they have the reins and clutch them tightly, not just around sharp turns, but also during the calm and smooth paths on their journeys. Though they may not recognize it, they are treating others just the way they believe they were treated in the past. It is like the abused child syndrome, where it is often abused children who become abusers themselves later in life. Likewise, overly controlling people often were overly controlled by others.

Consider the case of Harry, a new editor of a regional business publication. When he was a young man he learned the journalism ropes from his father, a prominent managing editor of a local newspaper. His father had very high editorial and ethical standards and was exacting with his staff (including Harry). Harry witnessed lots of micromanaging by his father, from having to approve every word written, every advertisement sold, and every source's credibility. When Harry joined his new firm as a manager himself, he drew on his father's approach as his model for managing his new staff. As you might imagine, it did not go over very well. Harry's over-controlling style angered his employees and even his own boss to the point that he lost several award-winning journalists to competitors because of it.

Being overly concerned with control often ensures that you prevail, at least for the moment, even if it means using manipulation, lies, and dishonesty. Unfortunately, it may also mean that you would do anything to get your way. But such behavior usually results in losing the power given to you by others, once your disingenuous behavior is recognized for what it really is—manipulation.

But what is manipulation at its core?

---

[1] James, W. (1902/1999). *The varieties of religious experience.* Reproduced by Modern Library Paperback, a division of Random House, Inc.

Manipulation Is Still Just Control

> Manipulation is a way to covertly influence someone with indirect, decep-
> tive, or abusive tactics. Manipulation may seem benign or even friendly or
> flattering, as if the person has your highest concern in mind, but in reality
> it's to achieve an ulterior motive. Other times, it's veiled hostility, and when
> abusive methods are used, the objective is merely power.[2]

Manipulation is a form of control, but it is an indirect form, and that is
what makes people who engage in it particularly irritating and difficult to
deal with. George K. Simon, in his book, *In Sheep's Clothing*, distinguishes between people who overtly try to persuade by aggressively fighting or bullying
others and those who, in his words, "… are subtle, underhanded or deceptive
enough to hide [their] true intentions … avoiding any overt display of aggression while simultaneously intimidating others … is most often the vehicle for
interpersonal manipulation."[3] At its core, manipulation is just *covert* control
over others.

Those who manipulate can only do so if we allow them to know our most
intimate fears. Manipulators generally use tactics that make just enough sense
to have us doubt our hunch that we are being taken advantage of or abused. In
addition, the tactics they employ keep us consciously on the defensive, and
they are highly effective psychological weapons to which anyone can be vulnerable. They include guilt, blame, bribery, emotional blackmail, sympathy,
and flattery. Unfortunately, our emotions often preclude us from recognizing
a manipulator's hidden agenda or motives.

It is hard to think clearly when someone has you emotionally on the run.
We all have weaknesses and insecurities that a clever manipulator might exploit. Sometimes we're aware of these weaknesses and how someone might
use them to take advantage of us. Sometimes we're completely unaware of
our biggest vulnerabilities. Manipulators often know us better than we know
ourselves. They know which buttons to push, and when and how hard to push
them. Bullying, both at school and at work, is one such example. Usually bul-
lies focus on our most vulnerable selves to exploit our weaknesses, especially
in front of others. Our lack of self-knowledge sets us up to be exploited and
to act like victims. Over time, we become victims of our own beliefs. Like the

---

[2] PsychCentral website, Lancer, D. (2017). How to spot manipulation. *Psych Central*. Retrieved October 3, 2018, from https://psychcentral.com/lib/how-to-spot-
manipulation/

[3] Simon, G. K. (2010). *In sheep's clothing: Understanding and dealing with manipula-
tive people*. Marion, MI: Parkhurst Brothers Publishers.

character Jordan Belfort explained in the movie, *The Wolf of Wall Street*, "the only thing standing between you and your goal is the bullshit story you keep telling yourself as to why you can't achieve it."

We all have seen or heard about organizational and political leaders who have tried throughout their careers to ascend to the top of their organizations, but who have slipped down the ladder because of <u>how</u> they achieved that goal. Those who desire control because they do not want anyone else to have it, or because they believe that only through controlling others can they achieve their own goals, have a distorted sense of what true leadership is.

Symptoms of Extreme Need for Control

At their core, overly controlling people do not know *who they really are*, because they have a distorted view of reality and do not see their own fallibility. People with a high need for control often

1. believe they have the answers to, and the responsibility for, everyone's problems (e.g., the "I, alone, can fix it" mentality),
2. become overly anxious working for others or delegating work to others (e.g., "No one can do this as well as me"),
3. become socially isolated, often being seen as egotistical and narcissistic,
4. are often oblivious to nonverbal cues from others, because they dwell at the center of their own universe,
5. become overwhelmed by problems, partially because they have perfectionist tendencies and procrastinate dealing with problems unless they have the perfect "fix," and partially because they deny the reality of what is really going on until it is too late to do much about it,
6. are overly defensive to the criticisms of others (i.e., they take everything personally) or they blame others when things do not go as planned, and
7. convince themselves that they are correct in taking control *because* of the response of others (e.g., lack of openness in communication, emotional or physical withdrawal, and lack of support).

Let's look at three of the more prominent ones: being a know-it-all, micromanaging others, and refusing to be held accountable or blaming others.

I Have the Answer to Your Problem

One of the most annoying tendencies of over-controlling leaders is that they believe they have the answer for everything. They are the "Mr. Fix-its" of our organizations and our lives. Moreover, they believe that they have the obligation and responsibility to solve everyone's problems.

Where does this come from?

First, these leaders do not always recognize their own fallibility, nor do they always see how situational contexts influence problems and solutions. For example, if they once have solved a problem a certain way, they believe that is the way to solve it—always. Even if the problem they encounter looks similar to one they've had or seen before, the situation is likely to be different.

Because they have a distorted view of reality (i.e., they see the world as a place that threatens their control), they attempt to maintain control by relying on the past successes they have had, even when the environment or the problem itself may have changed. As Albert Einstein so famously said, "We can't solve problems by using the same kind of thinking we used when we created them." One example of this is the focus on maintaining or bringing back jobs in the fossil fuel industry, despite the fact that science and economists suggest that more jobs will be created by expanding to cleaner energy approaches.

Second, overly controlling leaders have taken on solving problems so that they make sure they can implement whatever solution is adopted. In other words, if I come up with a solution, I probably understand it and what is required to put it into effect; therefore, I feel more in control. If, instead, you decide on the solution, I may not be able to actually do it, and that uncertainty threatens my control over the situation.

Third, they like being seen as a "Mr. Fix-it." It is validation for their egos (or, in some cases, denial of their fears). But seen in a more positive light, it can also be a way for them to connect to people through doing something they believe is helpful to others. It may be that providing solutions to others' problems is really speaking their own "love language."

The problem with trying to solve others' problems is that the solutions are not always the right solutions for that person. But a bigger problem is that this behavior takes away a chance for others to develop into good problem-solvers themselves. And, importantly, trying to "rescue" people from tough situations creates more victims—dependent children or dependent employees—which, in turn, leads to the next challenge: refusal to delegate and, ultimately, isolation.

I'll Do It Myself, By Myself

It is likely that most of you have been required at some point to work on a project with a micromanager. The scenario usually starts with an immediate suggestion by the person willing to take on the leadership role for the group. Usually everyone is fine with this in the beginning, since many of us don't want to be held responsible or accountable for everyone else's work, or we think that we don't have the time or resources to take on the job.

So far, so good.

Next come the task assignments, meeting scheduling, and the actual project work itself. However, it is usually the case that some people stop showing up at meetings; one or two members haven't turned in their work when expected; and there is always somebody who turns in garbage that has to be redone at the last minute.

One of the first tendencies is for the leader to micromanage every member so closely that, one by one, each ultimately gives up and relinquishes control to them. This abandonment of responsibility results in the very thing that is their justification for taking control in the first place: "No one but me can do this project right" or "Nobody is as committed to this as I am."

Following the unsuccessful attempt to get everyone on board, overly controlling leaders isolate themselves, refusing to work with other members who, after trying to find out where the project stands, give up and let the leaders have at it. The project result is generally not as successful, the members resent their leaders and each other, and the relationships among all the members deteriorate to the point that no one wants to work in a group ever again—especially the leaders! Then, if or when the product or process is questioned or criticized, the leaders are blind to the part they played in the debacle. This denial of responsibility results in another related challenge for leaders who are over-controlling: denial of accountability.

It's Not MY Fault!

As mentioned previously, overly controlling leaders often are oblivious to nonverbal cues from others and have narcissistic tendencies, primarily because they dwell at the center of their own universe. As a result, they become socially isolated. At their core, narcissists have an inflated sense of their own importance and a lack of empathy for others. But behind this mask of confidence lies a fragile self-esteem that's vulnerable to the slightest criticism.

Because overly controlling people take all criticism personally, they have the tendency to shift responsibility and accountability to other people or to the context. It is the classic fundamental attribution error: They rationalize their failures as due to external causes (e.g., people, situations, lack of resources, bad luck), but they attribute others' failures to internal causes (e.g., lack of ability, poor motivation, or inappropriate behaviors).[4] As a result, they do not accept the part they may have played in the unsuccessful endeavor.

Let's say your boss has a very high rate of turnover in her department. She may blame the amount of compensation she's able to offer, the poor quality of

---

[4] Ross, L. (1977). The intuitive psychologist and his shortcomings: Distortions in the attribution process. In L. Berkowitz (Ed.), *Advances in experimental social psychology* (Vol. 10). New York, NY: Academic Press.

applicants, or the lack of training available. What she probably doesn't attribute high turnover to is her own controlling management style. And yet, we know that most turnover tends to be higher in environments where employees feel they are taken advantage of, where they feel undervalued or ignored, and where they feel helpless or unimportant. In other words, often employee turnover is because of poor management and leadership. As is commonly stated, "People don't leave jobs, they leave managers."[5]

Working on Your Need for Control

By now it is apparent that for a leader with an extreme need for control the primary underlying fear is loss of control and that their primary response to that fear is trying to maintain control at all costs. If you have a tendency to have a high need for control, here is an exercise to help you focus on the underlying beliefs and motivations for your need to control:

1. For the next 2–3 weeks, describe in written form (e.g., a journal) some examples of the control problems, fears, and situations you experience in your work, school, and family relationships.
2. For each of the problems identified in Step 1, list the beliefs (causes) that account for your need for control.
3. Identify behavior, beliefs, attitudes, and feelings that need to be changed in order to resolve the problem.

Here's a more specific example:

- "At work today I was asked to completely change a report I worked on because my boss decided that she needed the information in a different format. Because I didn't want to change the report, I argued with the boss that the way I presented it made more sense."
- My belief is that if I know the "right" way to do something, I am not willing to do it in a different way just because someone in authority tells me to.
- I need to realize that I have to listen and consider someone else's opinion more openly. I must work on asking "why?" a requested change has me so defensive and work on identifying what I need to do to reduce my feelings of defensiveness.

---

[5] Higgenbottom, K. (2015). Bad bosses at the heart of employee turnover. *Forbes.* Retrieved February 17, 2017, from http://www.forbes.com/sites/karenhigginbottom/2015/09/08/bad-bosses-at-the-heart-of-employee-turnover/#6861589e4075

If You Work with Someone with a High Need for Control

If you work with someone or for someone with a high need for control, there are some helpful things to minimize the negative consequences for you:

1. Always remain calm and avoid aggressive language. Monitor the anxiety levels of the controlling person because it is usually under high levels of stress and anxiety when they most lose their coping skills. Offering to take something off their plate often helps calm them down.

2. Try respectfully approaching the person and explain that you understand and appreciate concerns for the project and getting good outcomes and that you want them, too. Then go on to explain how their controlling behavior affects you in terms of your own motivation.

3. When the controlling person does relinquish control, offer praise! Noticing the positive and acknowledging it may encourage them to want to do it again.

4. Recognize that sometimes the controlling person may not give you credit for your ideas or actions. This can be frustrating. However, sometimes for the "good of the order" it is better to have the solution than not to have it. Don't take it personally.

5. Finally, consider your own role in the person's controlling behavior. Have you done something (or failed to do something) that may have provoked such controlling behavior? Remember, all of us are prone to make fundamental attribution errors.

Here are some specific things you might say:

- "I see you are very worried about being able to complete Project X. I'm happy to do Task A for you so you can focus on Task B."
  or
- "When you ask me to give you my work so that you can rework everything, I feel like you don't trust me to use my experience and qualifications for the good of the project, and that makes me feel less motivated to do my best work."
  or
- "Thanks for trusting me with that task."

Now that we understand a bit more about leaders with extreme needs for control, let's turn our attention to the other need that can derail a successful managerial career: need for approval.

Need for Approval

The earliest relationships we have are with our parents and siblings. We learn to seek their approval for our behaviors, and to some extent for our feelings, at a very young age.

Why is this?

One reason is that we want to be loved, and so we may see disapproval of our *behaviors* as really showing disapproval of *ourselves*. Child development experts recommend separating these two (self from behavior) when providing feedback to children.[6] But for many people who grew up with parents or teachers who, intentionally or unintentionally, linked the two, others' disagreement or disapproval of their behavior is often viewed as disapproval of them as persons, unworthy of respect, dignity, and trust.

Several authors have demonstrated that individuals characterized by a high need for approval are more likely to conform to others' expectations and cultural values, and they are more easily influenced by others than those low in need for approval.[7] In essence, people with a high need for approval are protecting a vulnerable self-esteem. As adults, and especially as leaders, we need to learn to assume some responsibility for developing our own self-esteem without depending constantly on others to validate it. We need to recognize the potential for this phenomenon in our employees as well.

While the need for approval may be a natural evolution in our development, it can become problematic when we cannot get enough affirmation of our self-worth by solely relying on others to provide it. Sometimes, the problem develops because we don't get enough positive feedback from our parents, teachers, and peers. Receiving positive feedback helps us develop better social competence by motivating us to act in ways that encourage positive feedback to continue and by aiding our detection and accurate interpretation of social cues.[8]

However, there is a downside to having a view of self that is too positive. That is, if it isn't a realistic and true appraisal, we will not be as open to instruction and growth. Recent research, for example, has suggested that an extremely positive self-appraisal can sometimes be associated with poorer recall

---

[6] Rudolph, K. D., Caldwell, M. S., & Conley, C. S. (2005). Need for approval and children's well-being. *Child Development, 76*(2), 309–323.

[7] Cravens, R. W. (1975). The need for approval and the private versus public disclosure of self. *Journal of Personality, 43*(3), 503–514.

[8] Rudolph et al. (2005).

of negative events,[9] and this may result in a greater likelihood of distorting reality. For example, Justin A. Frank, M.D. discusses in his book, *Bush on the Couch: Inside the Mind of the President*, that President George W. Bush's "forgetfulness" about mistakes or actions in his past was likely due to his mother's overly positive (and, not necessarily, accurate) affirmation of him.[10]

Carol Dweck, in her book, *Mindset: The New Psychology of Success*,[11] describes two mindsets: fixed or growth. A fixed mindset is one in which talents and abilities are viewed as immutable. In other words, you are who you are, your intelligence and talents are fixed from an early age, and your fate is to go through life avoiding challenge and failure. A growth mindset, on the other hand, is one in which you see yourself as a work in progress. In essence, overly praising intelligence and ability doesn't foster a healthy self-esteem, nor does it lead to accomplishment, but can actually jeopardize one's success.

Sometimes, the feedback we get early in life from the people we admire is "improvement" feedback ("You need to get your grades up") or feedback that compares us with someone else ("What is with this "D" in math? Your sister never had trouble with math."). Negative or comparative feedback can be particularly distressing for those persons whose self-worth is threatened by disapproval, because they have a tendency to overreact to, or place a disproportionate emphasis on, such judgments.[12] For the most part, many of us tend to pay more attention to negative feedback than we do to positive feedback. Over time, whether the distortion in our reality is positive or negative, we will become accustomed to that distortion.

Consider the experiment in which college students were asked to wear special eyeglasses for 1 month that turned everything upside down.[13] At first, they stumbled around, tripped over things, and generally had great difficulty with perceptual judgment. Their brain knew how things were supposed to be and rejected what their eyes were telling them. But, after just a few days they adjusted, and their brains became accustomed to their upside-down world. After an entire month, the students reported that the glasses posed no challenge for them at all. In fact, they were able to navigate just as easily as

---

[9] Rudolph, K. D., & Pickett, C. L. (2004). *Need for approval and processing of social information*. Unpublished manuscript.

[10] Frank, J. A. (2004). *Bush on the couch: Inside the mind of the president*. New York, NY: HarperCollins.

[11] Dweck, C. S. (2006). *Mindset: The new psychology of success*. New York, NY: Random House.

[12] Rudolph, et al. (2005).

[13] Reported in McGraw, P. C. (2005). *Self matters*. New York, NY: Hyperion Press.

their right-side-up counterparts! Ultimately, they began to see this previously distorted view as perfectly normal.

The same phenomenon holds true with our acceptance of approval or disapproval from those who are important to us. Over time, approval causes us to build our positive self-view and feel worthy and valued. However, if we experience continuing disapproval, we begin to believe it and feel distress whenever we receive "constructive criticism" or when we realize that we are not meeting others' expectations. The distress is real, but the reaction is counterfeit. This distress often leads us to try too hard to please another, which becomes annoying or is perceived by others as "kissing up." It also provides us with a million excuses for past behavior, allowing us to play "the victim," never appearing responsible for our decisions. Neither of these responses is healthy.

Becoming overly reliant on others' feedback has taught us to become dependent on them, not just to gain their approval but also as models for what it means to be a "good" child, adult, parent, employee, or leader. One problem with this paradigm is that these models are often unrealistic or idealistic and can never really be emulated. Another problem is that we need to accept our strengths and challenges for what they really are, even if they are not "approved of" by others. Our realization that others may be better or worse than us at some things needs to be tempered by a similar recognition that we may be better or worse than they are at other things. This self-inventory is a solid foundation for recognizing the fullness of our potential for personal and professional development. The roadblocks to discovering this inventory, however, lie in our anxieties about, and fear of, disapproval.

No one likes to be shunned or ostracized. Particularly, no one likes to experience disapproval from someone we admire or love. And yet, none of us is immune to disagreements or questioning about what we think, how we behave, or whom we choose to support.

Remember that most approval needs begin early in our lives. As a result, we are conditioned to want to please those we love, partly for the emotional connection with them and partly for the realization that we are dependent on them for our very existence. From a child's viewpoint, this is perfectly normal. But from an adult's perspective, it is not.

Symptoms of Extreme Need for Approval

As a result of these anxieties and fears around disapproval, we tend to have a limited understanding of *who we really are*, because we are always trying to be something we are not or to behave in ways that lead to approval from others. As such, people with a high need for approval often

1. have low self-esteem,
2. give up on endeavors because they are convinced that whatever they do isn't "good enough,"
3. are emotionally dependent on others for affirmation,
4. avoid conflict because of the fear of others' disapproval of their views or to avoid hurting the feelings of others,
5. fret over the potential consequences of decisions to the point that they can never make a decision, and
6. fear rejection and abandonment so much that they subjugate their own needs, feelings, and wants to those of others.

When we encounter those who have an extraordinarily high need for approval we often feel uncomfortable with being so "needed" that we avoid, or even flee, relationships with them. We see that their unending requirement for positive strokes paralyzes their decision-making. We feel guilty, because we haven't given them enough reinforcement, or we feel overwhelmed by our perceived obligation to rescue them. And, occasionally, we feel sorry for them to the point of dismissing most of what they say and do as being based on their need for approval and not on what is *real*. Ultimately, however, we stop trying to "save" them, we lose respect for them, and we may end up having an emotional chasm in our relationships with them. The most ironic thing about people who are high in their need for approval is that they create the very thing that makes them most afraid—losing the approval of others.

Let's look at some of these symptoms in more depth so that we can begin to figure out how to engage with them in productive ways. There are many, but for now we'll focus on just three: low self-esteem, decidophobia, and fear of conflict.

I'm Not Good Enough

At the core of their fears is chronic low self-esteem. Self-esteem is based on the experiences you have had in life, and the messages sent by these experiences about who you are. Positive experiences tend to create positive self-beliefs. However, if our experiences have been negative, our beliefs about ourselves are likely to be negative, too.

Crucial experiences that help to form our beliefs about ourselves often occur early in life and are interpreted through the eyes of a child and, therefore, are often biased and inaccurate. Some of them were positive (e.g., receiving praise for good grades or exemplary behavior), but some of them were very negative (e.g., failing to meet parental or peer standards, being discriminated against because of your family or ethnic/racial group, experiencing an absence of praise or affection). Of course, negative beliefs about oneself can be caused by experiences later in life, too, such as workplace bullying or intimidation, abusive relationships, or traumatic events.

The problem with these previous and persistent negative experiences is that it causes those with extreme needs for approval to give undue weight to things that are consistent with these beliefs and to discount anything that is not. Basically this means that the focus is on what is <u>wrong</u> about them, ignoring what is right about them. They also have a tendency to distort meaning in what they do experience, even if that experience is positive. For example, getting a compliment about appearance might cause people with extreme approval needs to think that the person thought they were unattractive before or that the person is being disingenuous.

The result of low self-esteem is that an employees or managers do not believe they "deserve" any responsibility, rewards, or recognition. In other words, they believe they are undeserving, incapable, and not good enough to take on the task, hold the position, keep the relationship, or tackle the responsibility they've been given. That is why they are constantly seeking the approval from others to overcome their own perceptions of who they are and what they are capable of doing.

Whatever You Want Is Fine with Me

Making a decision requires confidence and a degree of certainty. And some decisions require a great deal of courage. When tough decisions with serious consequences are called for, it can be difficult for some people to act. The fear of making the wrong decision can cause a sort of mental paralysis; at its worst, it can ultimately create a phobia called "decidophobia"—the fear of making *any* decision.

For many people with extreme approval needs, this can be a common occurrence. The notion, "whatever you want is fine with me," really masks the underlying fear of making the wrong decision and, ultimately, losing the approval of others. Remember that it isn't that they don't care about the outcomes and consequences of the decision itself—they do. But the fear of disapproval overshadows the practical (and perhaps positive) results that the decision might have.

Take the situation faced by John F. Kennedy during the Bay of Pigs Invasion in 1962. The idea was to send in Cuban exiles to topple Fidel Castro. Kennedy called a special meeting to ask his top advisors whether he should authorize such an invasion. All concurred publicly, despite misgivings in the room. Each person in that meeting was unwilling to challenge it as a bad idea. One advisor even presented serious objections to the invasion in a memorandum to the president, but he suppressed his doubts at the meeting. The invasion was a disaster, primarily because no one was willing to go against what he thought was President Kennedy's desire.

By going along with what others want or refusing to decide at all, leaders with a high need for approval unrealistically believe they will avoid any unpleasantness, criticism, or conflict. Unfortunately, it is often the opposite result, creating more conflict and tension than if they had voiced a dissenting opinion. It is these interpersonal outcomes that are feared most and lead to the central plea: "Can't we all just get along?"

Can't We All Just Get along?

In essence, we all have a similar response to conflict: We don't like it. But, for someone who must have everyone's affirmation, an interpersonal conflict can be serious enough to cause anxiety and insecurity. When anxiety or insecurity is first experienced, as sentient human beings we have a choice between reactivity (i.e., flight or fright) and reflection. If we do not make a choice, our brain's default mode is to be reactive. From this anxiety and insecurity, we experience inadequacy (we don't know what to do) and a drop in self-esteem (we don't feel good about ourselves). And for someone with high approval needs, these experiences trigger the ultimate fear: loss of others' approval.

As a result, people who need a lot of approval and affirmation often choose to avoid conflict all together or to accommodate the person with whom they are having the conflict. Neither one of these is a healthy response, according to Kenneth W. Thomas and Ralph H. Kilmann, authors of the Thomas-Kilmann Conflict Mode Instrument (TKI).[14]

For starters, in conflict avoidance the person neglects both his own concerns and those of the other individual. Avoiding conflict might mean diplomatically sidestepping an issue, postponing dealing with an issue until a later time, or simply withdrawing from a conflict situation all together. As a result, leaders who routinely avoid conflict lose (or never gain) the respect of colleagues or direct reports, and, as a result, their perceived inability to confront interpersonal conflict eventually erodes their trustworthiness.

In accommodation, the person neglects his or her own concerns in order to satisfy the concerns of the other person. Basically, there is an element of self-sacrifice in this approach. Accommodating might take the form of obeying another person's order when one would prefer not to, or yielding to another's point of view, even when one doesn't agree. Although an accommodation

---

[14] Thomas, K. W., & Kilmann, R. H. (1974). *Thomas-Kilmann conflict mode instrument*. Mountain View, CA: Xicom, a subsidiary of CPP, Inc.

mode may garner some initial approval through its perceived cooperation with others, over time it is seen as indecisive and wimpy behavior, resulting in loss of confidence in the ability to stand up for oneself.

Working on Your Need for Approval

By now it is apparent that the primary underlying fear for leaders with an extreme need for approval is loss of approval from others and that their primary response to that fear is continuously seeking approval or avoiding disapproval at all costs. If you struggle with this yourself, here is an exercise to help you focus on the underlying beliefs and motivations for social approval:

1. For the next 2–3 weeks, describe in written form (e.g., a journal) some examples of the approval problems and situations you experience in your work, school, and family relationships.
2. For each of the problems identified in Step 1, list the beliefs (causes) that account for your need for approval.
3. Identify behavior, beliefs, attitudes, and feelings that need to be changed in order to resolve the problem.

Here's a more specific example:

- "At work today I was asked to completely change a report I worked on because my boss decided that she needed the information in a different format. I am sure she doesn't think how I did it is good enough."
- "The last time I turned in work my boss asked me to redo it because it had some errors. I'm sure she just said she needed a different format because I didn't do it right again."
- "I need to take my boss' words at face value. I must realize that "I am not the report" and that a critique of my work is not a critique of me, personally."

You might also try this:

1. Identify a person in your work life sphere and a person in your personal life sphere who you really want to think you are great.
2. For each person, list the characteristics they have that you most admire.
3. Now, for each characteristic you list, rate yourself on that characteristic (1 = Low, 5 = High). If you cannot be objective, ask a person close to you to rate you.

4. Develop a list of positive affirmation self-talk scripts you can use to affirm yourself on the highly-rated characteristics. Do not think further about the characteristics rated "low." Your task in this exercise is to work on understanding the relationship between what you value in others and your own perceptions of those characteristics in you.

If You Work with Someone with a High Need for Approval

If you work with a direct report, peer, or boss who has extreme approval needs, here are some helpful things to minimize the negative consequences:

1. Always remain calm and avoid aggressive language. Monitor the anxiety levels of the controlling person, because it is usually under high levels of stress and anxiety when they most struggle with questioning themselves.
2. Try respectfully approaching the person and explain that you understand and appreciate concerns for the project and getting good outcomes and that you want them, too. Then, remind them that you have every confidence that they can do the work. Offer any help or resources if they would like them.
3. When the work is turned in correctly, on time, and so on, thank them for their good work. Do not overly praise, but recognize the work itself (not the person). Noticing the positive and acknowledging it may encourage them to want to do it again.
4. Finally, consider your own role in the person's dependent or "victim" behavior. Have you done something (or failed to do something) that may have led them to fear your disapproval? Remember that all of us are prone to make fundamental attribution errors.

Concluding Thoughts

All of us have a need for control and need for approval, but when those needs are extremely high, our credibility and trustworthiness may be questioned. In the next chapter, we will look at the importance of being perceived as a trustworthy leader.

Additional Reading, Resources, and Activities

In order to get the most out of what you've already read and to see whether you are overly controlling or need a lot of approval and affirmation from others (or both), the following are some additional helpful resources and activities.

- Watch "The Devil Wears Prada," starring Meryl Streep and Ann Hathaway, to observe a "control-seeking" boss.

  - What challenges did the employees face having a controlling boss like Miranda Priestly?

  - Why do you think Miranda is so controlling? How is that demonstrated in the film?

  - Were there benefits to working for Miranda, despite her controlling approach? What were they?

- In contrast, to see the "approval-seeking" boss at work, watch one or two segments of the original British TV series, "The Office," starring Ricky Gervais as manager, "David Brent."

  - What challenges do employees have when their boss has a high need for affirmation as "David Brent" does?

  - How is David's need to be liked demonstrated in the segments you watched?

- Take the "Are You a Control Freak or Approval-holic?" assessment[15] on the next pages. Note where your highest score is and develop a plan to work on it.

---

[15] Dwyer, D. J. (2017). *Needy people: Working successfully with control freaks and approval-holics.* KDP Publishing, ISBN: 978-1973264538. Available on Amazon.com.

Are You a Control Freak or an Approval-holic?

Read each statement below and circle "T" if the statement is <u>generally</u> true for you and "F" if the statement is <u>generally</u> false for you. There are no right or wrong answers. Be as honest as you can.

T F	1.	If someone disapproves of me, I feel like I'm not very worthwhile.
T F	2.	It's extremely important to be liked by nearly everyone in my life.
T F	3.	I avoid making mistakes in front of others at all costs.
T F	4.	I believe I need the approval of others more than most people do.
T F	5.	I need others to approve of me in order to really feel good about myself.
T F	6.	It bothers me a lot to learn that someone doesn't like me.
T F	7.	If people I respect act disappointed in me, I dwell on it for days.
T F	8.	I seem to need everyone's approval before I can make an important decision.
T F	9.	I'm strongly motivated by the praise and approval I get from others.
T F	10.	I'm deeply concerned about what others think of me in most areas of my life.
T F	11.	I get very defensive when criticism is directed at me.
T F	12.	I need to have everyone like me, even though I don't really like everyone.
T F	13.	It only takes one person's criticism or disapproval in a group to upset me, even when everyone else is giving me praise.
T F	14.	I have trouble asking others for favors and tend to apologize a lot.
T F	15.	If I can control others, they will do what I want them to do.
T F	16.	I hate to feel out of control or to lose control.
T F	17.	I believe that if things don't go my way, I have to work harder.
T F	18.	It bothers me to have people see my true feelings, so I struggle to control my feelings in front of others.
T F	19.	I often step into a situation when I see something that needs to be fixed.
T F	20.	When I know in my own mind how something should be done, I work at trying to get it to be that way.
T F	21.	I am afraid that if I don't take care of something, it won't get done.
T F	22.	I tend to convey an "It's my way or the highway" approach with people who refuse to do something that needs to be done.
T F	23.	When I feel intimidated, I compensate by taking more control of the situation.

Source: Dale J. Dwyer

How to Score and Interpret Your Answers: Fill in the boxes below and total the number of "T" answers at the bottom of each column. (Higher scores indicate which is more problematic for you.) Then add both approval scores together and both control scores together to get "Total Approval" and "Total Control" scores.

Seek Approval	Avoid Disapproval	Control Self	Control Others
1.			
2.			
	3.		
4.			
5.			
6.			
	7.		
8.			
9.			
10.			
	11.		
12.			
13.			
	14.		
			15.
		16.	
		17.	
			18.
		19.	
			20.
		21.	
			22.
			23.
TOTAL APPROVAL (add above 2 scores)		TOTAL CONTROL (add above 2 scores)	

Source: Dale J. Dwyer

If your total Approval score is between 11 and 14, you have a high need for approval.

If your total Approval score is between 6 and 10, you have a moderate need for approval.

If your total Approval score is 5 or below, you have a low need for approval.

If your total Control score is between 7 and 9, you have a high need for control.

If your total Control score is between 4 and 6, you have a moderate need for control.

If your total Control score is 3 or below, you have a low need for control.

Manager as Leader:
The Importance of Being
Trustworthy

Three things are the sign of a hypocrite: when he speaks he tells lies, when he promises he breaks it, and when he is trusted he proves to be dishonest.

—*Islamic prophet, Muhammad, 570 CE – 632 CE*

In the *Republic*, Plato says that things will go well only when those who govern the state do not desire to govern. In other words, people who want to be in leadership roles are automatically suspect with regard to their intentions. The 19th century philosopher, Søren Kierkegaard, seems to agree:

> "Assuming the necessary capability, a man's reluctance to govern affords a good guarantee that he will govern well and efficiently; whereas a man desirous of governing may very easily either abuse his power and become a tyrant, or by his desire to govern be brought into an unforeseen situation of dependence on the people he is to rule, so that his government really becomes an illusion."[1]

One implication of these reflections is that unless leaders minimize their needs for control and approval, and their followers believe that they have truly done so, their motives for leadership are likely to be questioned, even if they make decisions or take actions that may appear beneficent. Or, as T.S. Eliot, in his work *Murder in the Cathedral*, put it, *The last temptation is the greatest treason: to do the right deed for the wrong reason.* Once their motives are questioned, the erosion of trust by their followers begins.

---

[1] Kierkegaard, S. (2010). *The Present Age: On the Death of Rebellion.* New York: Harper Perennial Modern Classics (originally published 1846).

The Importance of Trust in Leadership

Many scholars and theologians have written about the fundamental importance of trustworthiness in creating sustainable organizations and societies. For example, James Clawson and Michael Blank found that trust and respect accounted for a full 75% of the amount of learning and openness of the subordinate to influence from his or her leader.[2]

In the Bahá'í tradition this quotation from an early 4th century Persian tablet is most illuminating about the role of trustworthiness:

> Trustworthiness is the greatest portal leading unto the tranquility and security of the people. In truth, the stability of every affair hath depended and doth depend upon it. All the domains of power, of grandeur, and of wealth are illumined by its light.[3]

This statement is true in all organizational settings. Trustworthy leaders, co-workers, and followers become more secure in the tasks required of them and, in return, their loyalty and diligence provide stability for their organizations and civil societies. As Russell Hardin puts it, "The best device for creating trust is to establish and support trustworthiness."[4]

When we attain trustworthiness in the eyes of others, only then can we begin to create a sustainable organization or an enduring society capable of great things. That said, **trustworthiness might be the single most important factor in establishing and maintaining authentic leadership**.

But what does it mean to trust and to be trusted? How can people feel secure enough to put their welfare into the hands of others? There are several ways to understand the notion of trust: as encapsulated interest, as a cost-benefit calculus, and as interpersonal identification.

Trust as Encapsulated Interest

Political scientist Russell Hardin believes that much of what we call trust can be best described as *encapsulated interest*. Hardin would argue that we place our trust in those whom we believe to have strong reasons to act in our best interests. He writes,

---

[2] Clawson, J.G. and Blank, M.B. (1990). What really counts in superior subordinate relationships. *Mentoring International*, 4, 1, pp. 12–17.
[3] From the Fourth Taraz, gleaned from the Tablets of Baha'u'llah Revealed after the Kitab-i-Aqdas", p. 37
[4] Hardin, R. (1996). Trustworthiness. *Ethics*, 107, pp. 26–42.

It is this fact that makes my trust more than merely expectations about your behavior. Any expectations I have are grounded in an understanding (perhaps mistaken) of your interests specifically with respect to me.[5]

The "Encapsulated Interest" view implies that anyone whose interests are supposedly aligned with ours deserves our trust. Unfortunately, this perspective is not always accurate, as evidenced by the rash of corporate and political scandals that continue to plague the world. In these all-too-blatant instances of betrayal of trust, leaders say one thing and do another.

Think about your own boss. First, you will likely evaluate how actions that your boss takes will affect you, first and foremost, by what she says. Then, after she has acted, you probably decide whether or not she did what she said she would do. If she did, you are likely to have increasing confidence in what your leader says in the future and to trust that she will act similarly as she has in the past. If she acts contrary to what she had indicated, you will question whether you can trust what she says in the future.

Over time, your boss will become increasingly trustworthy if her actions are consistent with what she ultimately says and does. Of course, consistency with word and deed can also result in negative actions (e.g., "I said I would lay off 20% of the workforce, and I did"); from a trust perspective, however, her actions <u>are</u> consistent with her words, so you would likely believe her when she threatens layoffs in the future.

The bottom line is that to place trust in our leaders, we must see them as trustworthy. No matter how often they espouse their interests to be in line with our own (e.g., liberty and freedom, increased number of jobs, improved social conditions, organizational profitability, eradication of disease and poverty, etc.) we have difficulty believing untrustworthy people, primarily because their *behavior* differs so greatly from their *words*. We *hear* their stated positions, but we *see* budgets, policies, outsourcing, and removal or denial of liberties that don't support those positions. In sum, we begin to be distrustful of people when their words don't match their actions and when their interests and our interests appear incompatible.

Trust as a Cost-Benefit Calculus

Another view of trust is as a sort of *calculus* by which an individual is assumed to calculate the benefits of being in relationship with another person versus the costs of not being in relationship. In this view, trust will only be extended to another to the extent that the cost-benefit calculation indicates

---

[5] Hardin, R. (2002). *Trust and trustworthiness.* New York: Russell Sage Foundation, p. 2.

that an ongoing relationship with someone will yield a net positive benefit for the individual. Or, to put it another way, "I will trust you only if I believe that I will gain because of extending that trust to you," or "I will not trust you if I believe that the costs of extending that trust to you outweighs the benefits I will gain by doing so."

This view of trust is also grounded in one's judgments about whether the other person will behave predictably and reliably. Sometimes these judgments are flawed and based on false assumptions.[6] Similar to the encapsulated interest model, we determine whether we will trust someone based on the predicted outcomes for us—in this case, a continuing relationship.

It is also true that minor trust violations may result in reducing one's level of trust in one situation, but not another. For example, you may trust your manager to not reveal to coworkers that you are contemplating a divorce, but not trust him to make the decision to report one of his close peers for falsifying an expense report. As a result, because we have to continue to interact or work with our manager, the relationship becomes superficial and our behavior highly self-monitored.

Both the Encapsulated Interest and Calculus views are quite self-centered: we tend to extend trust to those who will benefit our interests or who will not harm us. Usually people holding either of these views are more concerned with how another's actions affect them personally and immediately, rather than the effect of their actions on the greater good for an organization in the long term.

For example, let's say that you distrust the CEO of your organization because he has begun outsourcing jobs to India. Are you focusing on the effect of that decision on your own individual job and livelihood? Are you ignoring more "big picture" outcomes, such as the broadening of economic markets (e.g., India) that should produce future demand for more products (not fewer) and a greater (not a lesser) need for U.S. talent as a result? Obviously, CEOs are in positions in which they are required to determine the effect of their actions in broader, more encompassing ways. Judging whether someone is a trustworthy requires us to look at the totality and sustainability of their decisions and behaviors on all stakeholders, not merely on the effect they have on any one individual or group during a finite and limited period of time.

A good example of this is a political leader. Political leaders often focus on their immediate constituencies, particularly during election times. Federal representatives from farm states make a big effort to show the number

---

[6] Lewicki, R.J. and Tomlinson, E.C. (2003). Trust and trust building. *Beyond Intractability*. Eds., Guy Burgess and Heidi Burgess. Conflict Research Consortium, University of Colorado, Boulder.

of times they voted for legislation that would benefit farmers, while those from industrial states emphasize their concern and support for manufacturing concerns. But the true test for the sustainable benefits of their decisions comes much later than a November election. In fact, history is replete with examples of "political" decisions that ultimately benefited no one but a politician's re-election campaign.

When deciding whether or not leaders are trustworthy, we mentally assign a measure of "trustworthiness" to them, based on how consistently, reliably, and equitably they have acted over time. Therefore, it is unlikely that we will trust leaders until they have demonstrated consistent and fair behavior across different situations with many different people.

Trust as Interpersonal Identification

Social scientists see trust and trustworthiness as more complex than calculations based merely on an alignment of interests or accrued benefits for individuals. For starters, we may perceive someone as trustworthy, but not actually act on that perception. This subtle distinction is the difference between making a relatively impersonal evaluation of another and our active investment in outcomes of relevant importance to us.[7] In other words, we can *say* that we trust someone, but until we *act* as if we do, followed by our evaluation of the outcomes stemming from those actions, we cannot know if our trust in that person was warranted.

This implies that we can only assess someone's trustworthiness retrospectively. Thus, the decision to trust another is based on our past experiences with them, but the actual feeling of trust is geared to our future behavior. Those individuals with whom we have ongoing and valuable relationships are more likely to garner our trust in the future than people who are merely acquaintances or with whom we have limited experience, just like the fox in the story of *The Little Prince*:

"What must I do to tame you?" asked the little prince.

"You must be very patient," replied the fox. "First you will sit down at a little distance from me—like that—in the grass. I shall look at you out of the corner of my eye, and you will say nothing. Words are the source of misunderstandings. But you will sit a little closer to me, every day ...." [8]

---

[7] Tanis, M. and Postmes, T. (2005). A social identity approach to trust: Interpersonal perception, group membership, and trusting behavior. *European Journal of Social Psychology*, 35, pp.413–424.

[8] de Saint-Exupéry, Antoine Marie Roger (1943). *The Little Prince*, Harcourt Brace Jovanovich, Inc.

This idea is supported by research suggesting that trust builds in stages, growing stronger and more resilient, and it changes in character.[9] That is, as a relationship grows through deeper understanding and repeated interactions, the individuals involved may become increasingly aware of shared values and goals. This allows trust to grow to a higher and qualitatively different level and begin to be a transforming experience for the relationship itself.

When trust evolves to the highest level, it is said to function as *identification-based* trust. At this point, trust has been built to the point that the parties involved have internalized each other's desires and intentions. They understand what the other party really cares about so completely that each party is able to act for the other. At this advanced stage, trust is also enhanced by a strong emotional bond between the parties, based on a sense of shared goals and values. They know that only the most grievous of behaviors can disrupt the bond between them, creating the feeling that no separation truly exists between them. So this view of trust, as a more emotionally-driven phenomenon, is grounded in perceptions of interpersonal care and concern.

Trust and Risk-taking

At this level of trust and trustworthiness, the beliefs held by one person about another's intentions, abilities, and integrity may lead them to take risks in their relationship by sharing information, taking on responsibilities, and working together on tasks. Self-disclosure, for example, requires risk-taking on the part of the person sharing information. That is, we generally don't self-disclose private thoughts and feelings to people we don't fully trust. Otherwise, we feel vulnerable, having given up some of our control to someone else and risking their disapproval of us.

We all have differing views on how to approach trusting others. Some of us start off trusting people and stop only if they prove that they are not trustworthy. Others of us are initially cautious, preferring not to trust until the other person proves to be trustworthy. Of course, there is no "right" or "wrong" way to approach the matter of trust; but it is worth remembering that each of us approaches this process differently, based on our own past experiences and comfort levels.

We also tend to trust others when we believe that they are still willing to learn and develop. This allows us to respect them and to treat them as we would ourselves, because we can see that they are aware of their own humanity, with all its pitfalls and frailties. It is seeing each other truthfully and

---

[9] See, for example, Lewicki, R. J., McAllister, D. J., & Bies, R. J. (1998). Trust and distrust: New relationships and realities. *Academy of Management Review, 23,* pp. 438–458.

authentically—not as heroes and geniuses, but as the recipients of responsible care and concern for others—that allows our trust to grow.

This becomes important for leaders to understand, particularly those who are beginning new relationships with followers. Consider Jim, for example, who was a close friend to several people at work prior to being promoted and becoming their leader. Their relationship as peers was based on relative equality regarding pay, authority, control, and other aspects of their work lives. But, when Jim was promoted into a leadership role, the relationship he had with his peers changed to one of less trust—even though he hadn't done anything differently or "untrustworthy" to warrant that change. Jim's peers merely awarded "trustworthiness" differently to peers than they did to their leaders, primarily because of their perception of risk in being vulnerable to their leaders. They typically trusted peers and only stopped trusting them if the peers proved untrustworthy; however, with leaders they were more cautious, withholding trust until the leaders proved trustworthy.

Amazing, isn't it? Even though Jim was the same person, his role as "leader" automatically made him less trustworthy among his former peers. And that is why Jim, the Leader, has to work to build the trust that Jim, the Peer, already had, because many followers assume that leaders, overall, do not share the same values and goals, cares and concerns that they do.

We attain trustworthy status by demonstrating that we are not substantively different from our bosses, peers, and direct reports, particularly in the values they hold dear. Because trustworthiness requires an emotional connection to achieve, becoming a trustworthy manager means recognizing that we have bonds that connect us with our colleagues, our customers, and our communities: a bond of shared goals, a bond of shared values, a bond of mutual respect. Managers who are able to attain trustworthiness in the eyes of employees must believe and act upon the premise that there is more that unites us than divides us as organizational citizens; to do otherwise, is to create mistrust, hostility, and separation.

The Roles of Approval and Control in Establishing Trustworthiness

But what keeps us from trusting others and acting trustworthy ourselves, if we buy into the premise that we are connected to each other? What prevents us from seeing the similarities, rather than the differences, we share?

Once again, our approval and control needs are creating the fear that distorts our views of each other and ourselves. These needs prevent us from becoming a trusting and trustworthy manager, peer, or co-worker.

First and foremost, *trusting behavior requires that we sometimes must relinquish complete control over processes and outcomes that are important to us.*

In order to develop trustworthiness, we must be willing to be vulnerable and humble. It is scary to be vulnerable and, to some people, humility is a sign of weakness. As we have discussed previously, the difficulty most people have in giving up control is that they become vulnerable to rejection and criticism. They are afraid to "let go," because they may end up responsible and accountable for their own mistakes and judgment, as well as for others' incorrect decisions.

Many of you may have experienced this with your boss. Does he or she typically micromanage your projects or refuse to delegate work to anyone? Does he or she tend to blame others or, at least, refuse to take blame for poor outcomes of decisions? If these sound familiar, it is likely that your boss also has a high need for control. He may also have a problem trusting others and, perhaps, is perceived untrustworthy by you and your colleagues.

Sometimes leaders also tend to avoid full emotional involvement with others by concealing their mistakes or distrusting others to do tasks. In this, they become vulnerable to their own *lack of trust in self,* which is deeply rooted in a need for approval. If leaders don't trust themselves, this is likely at the very heart of not being able to trust others.

Determining whether to trust others causes us to look for behaviors they exhibit that we approve of. Therefore, when we see behavior that doesn't fit our model of what a trustworthy person should do, we withhold trust until we observe different behavior that supports our model. We only begin to trust when we see behavior that, over time, confirms, rather than disconfirms, what we approve of.

Becoming More Trustworthy

So, what influences how trustworthy we appear to others or them to us? Three important questions provide clues:

- *Am I acting authentically?* Am I acting in a manner that is consistent with who I say and believe that I am? People who do not "walk the talk" and do not appear to be who they say they are will never gain the trust of others. It is often the disingenuous behaviors of leaders that undermines our trust of them.
- *Can I really do what I say I can do?* Am I competent in those things in which I profess to be competent? When we do not appear competent we will not gain trust, no matter what else we do or how much integrity we appear to possess.
- *Will I really do what I say I will do?* Is my actual behavior reliable and consistent with my promised behavior? People who say one thing and do quite another are usually perceived as untrustworthy.

Research has shown us that leaders who lack trust from followers tend to be angry, competitive, resentful, and lack empathy,[10] while leaders who are trustworthy tend to be happier, better liked by others, more honest, and more moralistic.[11] Trustworthy leaders do what they say they will do, and they never betray the confidence of those who trust them. To see where you currently stand on your own trustworthiness as a leader, take the *"Are You a Trustworthy Leader?"* quiz at the end of this chapter. Additionally, try giving it to someone who knows you well and see if that person agrees with you.

If gaining trust is determined largely by authenticity, competency, and the consistency and reliability of behavior, then how might this be demonstrated to others? What types of behaviors can we demonstrate that show others that we, indeed, are trusting *and* trustworthy? Here are a few suggestions:

- *Let others know your feelings, emotions, and reactions*; do not hide them because of fear, particularly of losing approval from others. These aspects of the real you are what forge the bonds of relationships. No one fully trusts those with whom they do not have a deep connection.
- *Place confidence in others* so that they will be supportive and reinforcing of you, even if you let down your "strong" mask and show your weaknesses. It's important for you to talk about your difficulties and mistakes from time to time. It makes you seem more human.
- *Assume that others will not intentionally hurt or abuse you*, should you make an error or a mistake. Otherwise, you will eventually become reclusive, isolated, and distrustful.
- *Let others into your life* so that you and they can create a relationship built on an understanding of mutual respect, caring, and concern to assist one another in growing and maturing independently.
- *Rely on others to treat you in a fair, open, and honest way.* If people act fairly and honestly, they will eventually experience similar behavior.
- *Do not act like a "victim."* You are in control of your choices, even if the consequences of your choices are not what you wanted or expected.
- *Create a healing environment* around you. Participate actively in forgiveness, understanding, and healthy communication to resolve problems and issues. Avoid blaming others; rather, encourage them to talk about their mistakes, just as you do.
- *Accept who you are* in the present moment. This is the real you, anyway.

---

[10] Gurtman, M.B. (1992). Trust, distrust, and interpersonal problems: A circumplex analysis. *Journal of Personality and Social Psychology*, 62 (6), 989–1002.

[11] Rotter, J.B. (1980). Interpersonal trust, trustworthiness, and gullibility. *American Psychologist*, 35, 1, 1–7.

As you begin to act trustworthy and to gain the trust of your peers, your followers, and your boss, you will be able to start the work of helping others to learn, grow, and change. As a result, you will be given more trust, responsibility, and influence in shaping the organizations you work for.

Concluding Thoughts

You should have some understanding of the complex role of "Manager as Leader," and you also have learned some of the reasons leaders fail at establishing trusting and meaningful relationships with their direct reports and colleagues. The next role we'll consider is "Manager as Change Agent," because all managers must learn how to move people and organizations out of their comfort zones.

ARE YOU A TRUSTWORTHY LEADER?[12]

Answer these questions as honestly as you can. If you have never been in a leadership role, ask someone else who knows you well to evaluate what they think you would do, based on their experiences with you to date.

1. Your company has recently sold a product line that will result in transfers, job reassignments, and possible layoffs for your group. In making these personnel decisions, will you:

   ○ A. Go to extremes to be fair and do the right thing, even if this is counter to the "company line"
   ○ B. Set up an evaluation process for everyone, except personal friends
   ○ C. Do what is politically correct and pleasing to top management

2. Customer demands require that one person in your department works on Christmas day. Will you:

   ○ A. Decide who will work based on who has the lowest seniority in the department
   ○ B. Offer to work unless someone else needs to work that day
   ○ C. Set up a rotation where everyone in the department, including you, the leader, will take a turn working this holiday

3. You have committed to helping your staff keep life and work in better balance by being more realistic in setting goals, priorities, and deadlines. What's the best statement about your behavior?

   ○ A. I will put forth a good effort but, with time, start to make exceptions
   ○ B. Sounds good, but the next time upper management and/or the client puts the heat on it will be back to "crunch" time and business as usual
   ○ C. Regardless of what happens, I will honor my commitments.

4. One of your employees received a lower performance evaluation and salary increase than expected. When they ask you to explain, you will:

   ○ A. Be forthright, honest, and truthful with the explanation
   ○ B. Be uncomfortable and tell only part of the reasons
   ○ C. Explain how you did not have full control over the decision

---

[12] Adapted from *Training & Development*, December 1997, 11.

5. Having just attended a farewell lunch for a close associate, one of your staff returns to the office and is called for a random drug test. The two glasses of wine punch at lunch (no surprise) leads to a small amount of alcohol detected. Will you:

   ○ A. Strictly adhere to company policy and put the staff member on a leave of absence

   ○ B. After a discussion, realize that this is a unique situation, exercise good judgment, and ignore the test

   ○ C. Recommend that the person enroll in the company's employee assistance counseling program

6. The first formal presentation of a junior staff member to the top management committee isn't going well at all. Will you, as her leader:

   ○ A. Jump in and ask for the presentation to be reschedule so "she can be better prepared"

   ○ B. Let her sink, and ask embarrassing questions, knowing that this is how lasting lessons are learned

   ○ C. Jump in to protect, support, and encourage her in a way that allows her to save face

7. There are rumors floating around about a significant change in direction and reorganization for your department. When asked by your staff, you:

   ○ A. Can be counted on to freely share all the information and ideas available

   ○ B. Will tell only what you think they need to know

   ○ C. Will discuss the changes only after they have been announced

8. You have been observed as a leader in a variety of situations. How would your staff describe what your behavior will be in an upcoming critical client meeting?

   ○ A. They haven't a clue, each day is a new day with you

   ○ B. Very predictable, there is little doubt in their mind how you will behave in various situations

   ○ C. Since this is a new client, they think they know how you will behave, but they are less than 60% sure of their predictions

9. Having known and worked with you for a number of years, would your staff say:

- ○ A. Your record is sporadic; sometimes you could be trusted, sometimes not
- ○ B. Knowing what they know about you, there is no way they would trust you
- ○ C. History indicates that you can be trusted implicitly

10. A decision needs to be made that will have a huge impact on the direction of your department. Will you:

- ○ A. Respect and treat each person as an equal partner in making this decision
- ○ B. Consult with and listen to others' input then make the decision yourself
- ○ C. As the boss, analyze the facts in the situation, seek little input, and then make the decision you think is best

Scoring

1. A=10, B=5, C=2	Implementing and abiding by procedures that treat everyone fairly will increase the trust others have in you. Not showing favorites and being willing to take a stand for fairness are critical elements of this dimension of trust.
2. A=2, B=10, C=5	How concerned are you with the goodwill and interests of others? Actions that place their self-interests before yours are strong indicators of your genuine concern and sensitivity to their self interests.
3. A=5, B=2, C=10	Can you be counted on to keep your commitments in both the good and bad times? You can't trust someone who says one thing and does the other or when pressured, conveniently forgets commitments.
4. A=10, B=5, C=2	How would others rate your integrity? Two key elements in their conclusions would be your reputation for honesty and truthfulness even when this might be uncomfortable. How could others trust someone who is dishonest or tells only half-truths.
5. A=2, B=10, C=5	Your consistency, reliability, predictability, and good judgment in handling situations will tell others that you can be trusted. Do you temper all of this with good judgment? Can you be counted on to "do what is right" even in the face of contradictory circumstances?

6. A=5, B=2, C=10	Other's trust in you will increase if they see you as loyal and willing to protect, support and encourage them. Exhibiting caring compassion and running interference, allows you to experiment in an environment that is non-threatening to your self-image.
8. A=5, B=2, C=10	Are you predictable, reliable, and responsive in a caring way? How can other trust someone whose actions are random?
9. C=10, A=5, B=2	An indicator of how much trust others can place in you is your track record. History does repeat itself. Ask yourself if the evidence supports the case for others trusting you.
10. A=10, B=5, C=2	Trust is reciprocal. Through your words and actions, do you openly show others that you trust and respect them when it really counts? If you don't trust them, how can you expect them to trust you?

Your score

80–100	Your actions are consistent regardless of the person, place, or event. You care for others, are consistent, do the right things regardless of personal risk, and exude integrity. Congratulations, others find working with you a unique and rewarding experience.
50–80	Your closest confidants can trust you, others are not sure—sometimes yes, sometimes no. The word is consistency. Seek out and change those actions that are sending mixed signals if you want higher levels of trust from others.
20–50	You probably find others become quiet when you walk in the room, seem to weigh their words, and begrudgingly share information with you. You often feel lonely, but the good news is that you can change. Look over the quiz and ask how you can start to behave in a more trustworthy fashion.

Manager as Change Agent

The painter should not paint what he sees, but what will be seen.

—*Paul Valery, French Poet (1871–1945)*

You may have heard it said that there is no constant but change, and it's true. All managers must learn how to marshal the resources—human, financial, operational—to create and implement changes, large and small.

At times a manager may be more interested in organizational-level changes, such as moving from a very bureaucratic, process-focused culture to a more entrepreneurial, innovative culture. Or, because of improvements to equipment or machinery, employees may need to start using different technologies. Other changes may be at the individual level, for example, making improvements in customer service or attendance behavior. These are merely examples of a host of changes organizations may be facing, either by choice or by necessity. Interestingly, although each type of change requires different approaches, diagnostics, and interventions, they do have some common requirements. As a result, each kind of change requires something different of the manager-change agent and, thus, different types of changes require different management competencies.

This chapter is not intended to be a complete treatment of all the methods for diagnosing change needs, designing possible interventions, or putting into place evaluation measures. Rather, it is intended to help you know what competencies you need to develop in order to lead and manage change in the organization. Part of this self-assessment is in knowing how you are inclined to think about change and how consistent you are in your approach during change processes.

Living in the Vision

One of the mistakes made by many managers, both new and experienced, is a tendency to be so passionate about changing or improving something that they begin the entire process too quickly and take on too much at once. Although they "see" the change or the outcome of the change in their own minds, they do not envision what the picture will look and feel like to others, how long it will take to create, and how to sustain improvements over time.

This isn't really surprising. Usually, managers have been thinking about the change for quite some time before they bring others into the picture. For example, I remember before I built my house, I put the initial house plans up in a prominent location in my apartment. I envisioned walking through the house, figuring out where to put dishes and cooking utensils in the kitchen, arranging the furniture in the various rooms, and imagining how other daily activities would be done there. Every day, for several weeks, I practiced "living" in the house. Eventually, I made changes to the plans to accommodate a problem or two that I discovered in this process. When I finally moved in, it already felt like home.

When employees hear an idea for the first time, their leaders have already spent a lot of time thinking about the change with all of its potential pros and cons, what will be required, who might be involved, resources that might be required, and so on. In other words, they have "lived" in the vision before they present it, virtually fully formed, to their followers. This usually results in managers being shocked that their employees don't see what they see.

In addition to moving too quickly through the conceptualization phase, managers often have difficulty conveying the vision to organizational members, because the ideas underlying the vision are complex and difficult to explain in words. They try to overcome this complexity by only conveying parts of their idea at any one time, or they may try to convey just an overview in a single meeting. This approach may backfire, because employees, who are not yet able to see and understand the entire picture, wonder what they are missing and what is being kept from them.

Despite these well-intentioned approaches, leaders are often unable to convey the picture very clearly or completely, leaving employees confused and unclear about the need for the change, the outcome expected, the process to be used to achieve the change, their role in working on and accomplishing the end result, and the impact of the change on everyone's daily jobs and tasks. And when employees are confused and unclear about what the leader wants, they plant their feet and refuse to budge.

As my grandmother used to say, "More haste, less speed." That is, the more quickly a leader tries to implement a change, particularly if it is a large one, the slower and the less successful the entire process becomes. Likewise, the more confusing and complex the vision of the change and the explanation given for its purpose and implementation, the more resistant employees become.

Given that many managers attempt change too quickly and often convey an unclear picture of the planned change, it is not surprising that most employees have a history of unpleasant experiences regarding how their organizations have attempted change in the past. Such misguided approaches to change result in employees neither understanding nor experiencing the change in the same way the manager has envisioned it. And, thus, the manager mistakenly attributes employees' resistance to fear of change or just plain stubbornness.

In reality, part of the resistance is due to the fact that everyone has a different perception about the change itself as well as the reasons for that change. In fact, most employees (and in some cases, the managers themselves) resemble the blind men and their experiences with an elephant, as recounted in this poem by the American poet, John Godfrey Saxe (1816–1887)[1]:

The Blind men and the Elephant

It was six men of Indostan
To learning much inclined,
Who went to see the Elephant
(Though all of them were blind),
That each by observation
Might satisfy his mind.

The First approached the Elephant,
And happening to fall
Against his broad and sturdy side,
At once began to bawl:
"God bless me! But the Elephant
Is very like a wall!"

The Second, feeling of the tusk,
Cried, "Ho! What have we here,
So very round and smooth and sharp?
To me 'tis mighty clear
This wonder of an Elephant
Is very like a spear!"

The Third approached the animal,
And happening to take
The squirming trunk within his hands,
Thus boldly up and spake:
"I see," quoth he, "the Elephant
Is very like a snake!"

---

[1] Saxe, J. G. (1881). *The poems of John Godfrey Saxe* (Highgate Edition). Boston, MA: Houghton Mifflin.

The Fourth reached out an eager hand,
And felt about the knee.
"What most this wondrous beast is like
Is mighty plain," quoth he:
" 'Tis clear enough the Elephant
Is very like a tree!"

The Fifth, who chanced to touch the ear,
Said: "E'en the blindest man
Can tell what this resembles most;
Deny the fact who can,
This marvel of an Elephant
Is very like a fan!"

The Sixth no sooner had begun
About the beast to grope,
Than, seizing on the swinging tail
That fell within his scope,
"I see," quoth he, "the Elephant
Is very like a rope!"
And so these men of Indostan
Disputed loud and long,
Each in his own opinion
Exceeding stiff and strong,
Though each was partly in the right,
And all were in the wrong!

So, what's a manager to do?

As we have already discussed, ensuring that your employees see you as trustworthy goes a long way when creating a change-ready organization. But, even then, changes that are too large, too confusing, and too fast will lead to many issues, including loss of excellent employees, mass confusion, and resistance throughout the organization. Such an approach also challenges the manager's credibility by raising questions in employees' minds concerning the feasibility of the proposed changes. It is also likely that the changes will not be sustainable in the long run because employees will not fully understand what is desired or required. A second key, then, is to create a vision for your followers so that they not only intellectually understand the vision but also experience it. In other words, it is crucial that people employ their senses, in addition to their intellect, so they truly embrace the changes you are asking them to make.

Creating an Experiential Vision

There is a difference between thinking about something and experiencing it. In 1972, there was a horror movie, *The Last House on the Left*, that used the promotional hook, "It's only a movie," in its advertisements. Viewers got so emotionally caught up in the images and violence they saw on the screen that they were apt to forget that it was "only a movie." Although they might have known, intellectually, that it was fiction, when they were in a darkened theater watching the images and listening to the music and sounds, they experienced the movie's *sense appeal.*

What is sense appeal? All of us continually experience the world through our five senses. When we are able to enter into an event so fully that the senses are able to muster emotions appropriate to that event, just as if we were actually going through it, the event will be more memorable, personalized, and understandable. That is sense appeal: the ability to draw upon the five senses to engage people in an *experience*, not just in an intellectual exercise. Most likely, anyone who saw that movie never forgot it or the emotions it aroused.

You probably have had similar experiences with a movie, song, perfume, or food. We are inclined to remember and personalize those strong experiences so fully that we are able to call them back and relive them almost on demand. If you want people to think about something, you use words, concepts, and cognitions. But if you want them to experience it, you need visual images, metaphorical language, music, aromas, and anything else that engages their senses.

Think about some of our most revered images, sounds, and smells, and the experiences they represent. For example, holiday tree lights, stars, angels, candles, crèches, menorahs, and other symbols help us to express the deepest meanings of our religious holiday season. To create an emotional attachment to a home for sale, we often entice potential buyers with the smell of hot bread or cinnamon and the warmth of candlelight and crackling fires. A particular perfume or cologne may remind you of someone you previously dated (of course, this could be a good thing or a bad thing!), and a song that was popular when you were in high school takes you right back to events and relationships from those days. Symbols, visual images, aromas, and music intensify experiences by recalling memories, stories, events, and relationships that have come to have deep meaning for us.

Asking employees to think about a vision involves dissecting it into pieces for clarification and analysis in some impersonal, objective way. Such an intellectual and cognitive exercise leaves them cold and uninspired. But when you ask them to experience the vision, the process of experience involves not only their minds but also their bodies and emotions. In organizations, we often expect people to back emotion out of their thinking processes, to keep their emotional distance and objectivity. We make the assumption that people can't be objective and respond emotionally at the same time, and we also usually praise them for their objectivity. But all of us can respond with emotion and feeling *and* still make objective business decisions that are in the best interests of the organization.

Consider the story of Malden Mills and its leader, Aaron Feuerstein. Malden Mills is the maker of the innovative fabric known as Polartec. On December 11, 1995, a fire burned most of Malden Mills to the ground and put 3,000 people out of work. Most of the 3,000 thought they were out of work permanently. A few employees were with Feuerstein in the parking lot during the fire and heard him say, "This is not the end." And it wasn't. Aaron Feuerstein spent millions of his own money keeping all 3,000 employees on the payroll with full benefits for three months while they rebuilt the factory. Why? Because Feuerstein made his decision with both his head and his heart. As he noted, "I have a responsibility to the worker, both blue-collar and white-collar. I have an equal responsibility to the community. It would have been unconscionable to put 3,000 people on the streets and deliver a death blow to the cities of Lawrence and Methuen. Maybe on paper our company is worth less to Wall Street, but I can tell you it's worth more." He was willing to put his money, reputation, and business on the line to move the company forward in a changing, risky business climate. And this decision created another fire— one within his employees—for a vision of a new, better-than-ever, Malden Mills. In a newspaper interview much later, Feuerstein remarked, "Before the fire, that plant produced 130,000 yards [of material] a week. A few weeks after the fire, it was up to 230,000 yards. Our people became very creative. They were willing to work 25 hours a day."[2]

As you create and attempt to convey your vision, remember that if it doesn't stir senses, it will be perceived as boring, and it probably won't ever be realized. Boring visions don't engage employees to create, innovate, and grow. No doubt you've all experienced a boring lecture, an uninspiring sermon, or a run-of-the-mill project assignment. Think about what made them boring, uninspiring, and dull. It wasn't the amount of intellectual content or how much thinking you had to do. Rather, "boring," "uninspiring," and "dull" connote the lack of the five senses being stirred, and this prevented you from experiencing the class, the worship service, or the project to their fullest

---

[2] Desjardin, J., & Hartman, L. (2008). *Business ethics: Decision-making for personal integrity and social responsibility.* New York: McGraw-Hill.

extent. Furthermore, we cannot be fully present in the midst of a meaningful and exciting experience or relationship without sense appeal.

What are the elements that need to be present for employees to truly experience a vision? First, images and metaphorical language that appeal to one or more of the five senses are critical to being able to experience a vision. Such use of sense appeal leads to employee identification so that they can see themselves in the vision. Once identification occurs, employee emotion is stirred so that they feel connected to the vision. As emotion is stirred, employees become interested and engaged in the improvement or change so that they commit to the vision. And when employees have interest, they listen and are open to the possibility for improvement and change in themselves as well as in the organization. Thus, visions that have more sense appeal create more interest, and this, in turn, creates opportunities and increases the possibility that people will be less resistant to change and want to participate in making it a reality.

The leader's job, then, is to create ways that help people use their senses to touch, feel, taste, hear, and see—in other words, *experience*—the vision. Leaders need to develop their abilities to be sense-descriptive and imaginative. Very few people are gifted at this, and most of us must work to develop it. Let's look at some ideas to help you become more adept at creating sense appeal for your vision.

- **Search first for the meaning in the vision, rather than the words that describe it.** Many organizations spend an inordinate amount of time on the wording of a vision statement, rather than the meaning underlying it. I can remember the endless wordsmithing that went on during the crafting of the first vision statement for our college. Many of the faculty still joke about the amount of time the strategic planning committee spent on the wording, particularly whether to say we were "a scholarly community" or "a community of scholars." The crucial point, of course, was to capture the underlying meaning—in this case, that we saw ourselves as a community of persons dedicated to all that was involved in discovering and disseminating knowledge. The point is that you must get the meaning of the vision clear in your own mind first. Only then can you paint the vision with all its messiness until others can see it, feel it, and describe it accurately. Once the vision is clear to you, finding the descriptive words will be easier and less controversial. For example, read the following vision and try to experience what it would feel like to be a part of it. Before you read further to see whose vision it is, try drawing a picture of what you see and putting down some words that describe the emotions you might feel:

It will be a place for people to find happiness and knowledge. It will be a place for parents and children to spend pleasant times in one another's company: a place for teachers and pupils to discover greater ways of understanding and education. Here the older generation can recapture the nostalgia of days gone by, and the younger generation can savor the challenge of the future. Here will be the wonders of Nature and man for all to see and understand ... [it] will be based upon and dedicated to the ideals, the dreams, and hard facts that have created America. And it will be uniquely equipped to dramatize these dreams and facts and send them forth as a source of courage and inspiration to all the world ... [it] will be something of a fair, an exhibition, a playground, a community center, a museum of living facts, and a showplace of beauty and magic. It will be filled with the accomplishments, the joys and hopes of the world we live in. And it will remind us and show us how to make those wonders part of our own lives.

If you wondered which organization this vision belongs to, it's Disneyland. Its creator, Walt Disney, was a genius at painting a compelling picture. When he started his theme park, he was clear on its purpose, "We're in the happiness business." Disney saw it as a very different purpose from being in the theme park business. In addition, this vision was expressed in the charge he gave every cast member: "Keep the same smile on people's faces when they leave the park as when they enter." He didn't care whether a guest was in the park 2 hours or 10 hours. His goal was to keep them smiling. The vision you just read certainly captures Walt Disney's meaning, and it still captures what takes place in Disney theme parks every day, don't you think?

- **Look around you for ideas, pictures, and icons to use.** Most of you won't have to look very far to find ways to relate your vision to the everyday lives of your followers. You can use current events, cultural icons, popular media, or ongoing relationships. Organizations that make the most of sense appeal capture those things that bring back fond memories, have instant recognition, and excite the imagination. They are able to find the link to what people already know, understand, and have experienced. The key is to chisel what you find every day into usable messages, pictures, and events that have meaning and are likely to be remembered and repeated by a majority of employees, primarily because the meaning and the identification are readily known and familiar to them. Adopting a television show as the model and process for refining a vision (e.g., *American Idol, Survivor*) will create participation from a broader group of employees. Anything that engages people is fodder for you to use, and the more familiar it is, the more memorable and engaging the vision and visioning process will become.

- **Try using reverse psychology.** Employees, particularly ones who have been through numerous "fad of the month" changes, expect that the vision you introduce will just be more of the same. They are waiting for this vision to pass so they can go back to the familiar. When you employ reverse psychology, employees expect one thing but get something else. For example, try a vision that describes the organization in terms that are very different than the traditional jargon. Hospitals have often done this by using terms that apply more to hotels than medical facilities. Or, try something that is so far-reaching that people will stop dead in their tracks at first. Make it as ludicrous as you can. Then ask them to explain why they believe that vision is so ludicrous or unachievable. Once their anxiety abates, you can then engage with them in a fresh encounter to create a more reasonable, but still exciting, possibility.

- **Remember that your role is one of translation.** People don't think about the world in intellectual and philosophical categories. They don't use abstract language when they are trying to convey an idea that matters. Using traditional "vision language" is like speaking Aramaic or Latin; it is a dead language for 21st-century people. How many of us really understand what is meant by, or see how we fit into, a vision that says, "To be a world-class telecommunications company," or "To be widely recognized as the premiere provider of innovative financial products and services"? As leaders, our task is to use sense appeal to allow people to receive and understand our message. A vision will only appeal to everyday people if it is stated in everyday language that has description and meaning for them. Your role in this process is to build a bridge between the present and the future. Employees want a bridge builder who helps them understand how they get from where they are to where they need and want to be. Martin Luther King, Jr., was such a leader; he was able to translate his vision of equality to hundreds of thousands of people through metaphorical language, emotion, and his own actions: "I have a dream that my four children will one day live in a nation where they will not be judged by the color of their skin but by the content of their character." Work on becoming a translator, and your vision, as well as the means to realize it, will be more clearly accepted, understood, and experienced.

Four Types of Changes

While you may have a compelling vision for a different tomorrow, there are many types of change that require different approaches and, thus, different leader competencies. To paraphrase George Orwell in his book, *Animal Farm*, "All change is equal, but some changes are more equal than others." That is, change generally means moving the organization from one state of affairs to another (i.e., outcome), but it can also mean changing processes, systems, structure, people, culture, and products or services.

Some organizational-level changes will be incremental and static in nature; that is, doing something differently will change in baby steps, but once it's done, it's done. This is referred to as *discontinuous* change. Changes in employee reimbursement forms or a reimbursement process would be incremental and static changes.

Some changes will be incremental, but dynamic, that is, changes that require a longer time period. Here, we might use the example of a change in an organization's employee benefits registration process, from a paper-based system to a 24-hour web-based system. This type of change would require incremental and transitional steps over perhaps a year or two, when the changed employee registration process would ultimately be completed and ready to use. But it is dynamic, or what we refer to as *continuous*, because continuing technological advances will require additional changes as new technology becomes available.

When an organization changes in more quantum and static ways, it usually is a large, one-time (sometimes negative) event, such as downsizing or divesting itself of a major product, service, or division. On the more positive side, changes can involve putting out a new product, offering a new service, or hiring a new management team.

Finally, mergers, acquisitions, and spin-offs are examples of quantum and dynamic organizational changes that take a long time to finalize and require a lot of buy-in and participation from everyone. Like macro-level organizational changes, micro-level individual employee changes can also be incremental or quantum, static or dynamic.

One way to think about the differences in how we approach change is to consider how we change our hairstyles. Let's say that you have short hair. If you want to grow your hair long, it takes a long time and requires constant shaping (dynamic and continuous) until you get it to the length you want it. Moreover, you only gradually notice the change occurring (incremental). It is usually an uncomfortable process, and sometimes you may decide you just can't put up with it anymore and go back to a shorter style. But if you have long hair and decide you want it short, you can accomplish it in one day (static and discontinuous) and the change is quite definitive and noticeable (quantum). The downside is that you can't go back to long hair unless you engage in an incremental, continuous process.

In organizations, each type of change requires different competencies of the leader and different activities for organizational members. In the next section, we'll look at how you might discover the type(s) of change for which you are already skilled and those for which you are not currently very skilled. Incidentally, very few managers will be equally adept at all four of these types. Learning when you need to bring in others to complement your own abilities is crucial to ensuring your credibility as a change agent, as well as increasing the likelihood that your change and improvement efforts will be sustainable.

Different Approaches for Different Types of Changes

In their book, *Learning to Change*, Léon de Caluwé and Hans Vermaak ingeniously identify five approaches to change by assigning them colors: yellow, blue, red, green, and white.[3] Each of these typifies a focus for the change and some underlying assumptions about how people and organizations change. Each requires different competencies for those leading and implementing the change. None is necessarily better than the others, but you will probably see yourself as resonating more with one than with the others. Knowing which you are more likely to adopt may help you understand why employees who are unlike you may be resistant or afraid of the approach you take. According to de Caluwé and Vermaak,

- *Yellow-print thinking* focuses on uniting the interests of stakeholders, sometimes by negotiations and sometimes by invoking power position.
- *Blue-print thinking* focuses on planning and controlling the change through structure, planning, and goals.
- *Red-print thinking* focuses on employing human resource tools in an effort to get the best from the people who will be implementing the change.
- *Green-print thinking* focuses on learning with and from others, a process that ultimately leads to changed mindsets and behaviors.
- *White-print thinking* focuses on identifying patterns that, over time, have contributed to the status quo and that need to be changed for a new organization to emerge.

If you see the three lenses (strategic design, political, and cultural) in these, good for you!

Like the three lenses, these "colors" mean different ways of looking at what is important during change initiatives, and they also mean that different approaches and competencies will be required of the leader. Depending on which of the four types of change is desired, some of these approaches work better than others. Let's look at each of the four types of change, likely approaches to use, and what may and may not be required of you as the agent of change.

---

[3] de Caluwé, L., & Vermaak, H. (2003). *Learning to change.* Thousand Oaks, CA: Sage.

Incremental and Static (Discontinuous) Changes

Clearly, the biggest measure of success for incremental, static changes is that they get done in a timely manner with as little disruption to the daily business of the organization as possible. However, incremental and static changes usually don't affect the core mission, product, or service of the organization. And even when they do, the small change that occurs doesn't normally affect the daily routine of employees or the organization. Believe it or not, many such changes may even be welcome if they help employees do their jobs better!

Because this type of change is done in small steps, and because we try not to disrupt people (e.g., employees, customers, vendors) while we are implementing it, *blue-print thinking* (or, in our terms, a strategic design lens) is usually the preferred approach. It invokes structure and planning on the part of the change agent. Because it is a one-time event, the more planning that occurs upfront, the less hassle it becomes during the implementation phase.

It is not inconceivable that if the change, albeit incremental, requires a lot of buy-in from employees; you may need to adopt a bit of the red-print or green-print approach, too. Using rewards, training, coaching, feedback, and other employee-centered tools may help in the adoption of the change. But, by and large, the quicker and the less painful the change is, the better for everybody.

The strategic design or blue-print thinking requires the following competencies from the change agent:

- Analytical thinking
- Goal setting
- Focusing on results
- Setting and meeting deadlines (time management)
- Clearly communicating expectations
- Planning and organizing
- Linear thinking (i.e., thinking in discrete units and in logical order).

Incremental and Dynamic (Continuous) Changes

The very nature of a dynamic change suggests that it keeps going for a while. By and large, the dynamism of change is what is both frustrating and comforting at the same time. It's frustrating, because it feels as if it will never end. Just when we think we've got it, more tweaking is required. It's comforting, though, because we can take the time to experiment, make mistakes, and fix it. And because this type of change is incremental, we can see the results of the changes so we know what is working and what needs our attention.

Blue-print thinking and strategic design is also important for this type of change because of the planning, analysis, and time management issues involved. But incremental and dynamic change initiatives also require more attention to the people issues and, especially, the learning cycle. The importance of having a balanced and realistic approach to individual and organizational learning during a dynamic change process cannot be underestimated. Thus, managers who are able to embrace green-print thinking, in addition to blue-print thinking, will be much more successful over the duration of the change.

Thus, in addition to blue-print thinking competencies, leaders embarking on incremental and dynamic changes also need green-print thinking competencies:

- Coaching and teaching skills
- Patience for individual learning styles and pace
- Focus on learning (i.e., willingness to make mistakes, receive constructive feedback)
- Respect for others' points of view
- Facilitation skills
- A beginner's mind (i.e., getting rid of preconceived notions)
- Tenacity and persistence (i.e., not giving up in the middle).

Quantum and Static (Discontinuous) Changes

You don't have to look very far to see the impact that a quantum, static change has. Most of the ones we're familiar with are the negative ones that we see in the media. Plant or school closings, mass employee layoffs, restructuring, corporate scandals, bankruptcies, and product liability litigation are commonly large, one-time events that have devastating effects on organizational and civic communities. At the very least, they are public relations nightmares. However, some quantum changes are positive, like the opening of a new plant or organization, the introduction of a new product or technology, or the discovery of a new medical treatment.

All of these examples have a few things in common. For one, successful quantum, static changes by their very nature disrupt the flow of business and people's lives. These can feel just like a natural disaster—a tornado, earthquake, or fire. One minute things are fine, the next minute they aren't. They most always affect the core mission, the product or service, and the employees of the organization. For another, whether perceived as a positive or a negative event, quantum, static change requires leaders who are not only politically savvy but also are sensitive and responsive to the people who are most affected by, or who are able to affect, the change. For this reason, both yellow-print thinking and red-print thinking are extremely important approaches for this type of change.

Yellow-print thinking (or the political lens) is concerned with making sure that the political coalitions are in line so that the common interests of the people are united or, at least, they are perceived to be common and united. The management of a quantum, static change requires a great deal of negotiating and compromising in order to see an eventual successful outcome—one that might be considered to be a win-win for both the organization and the employees.

Yellow-print thinking and the political lens requires the following competencies:

- Political savvy
- Ability to negotiate and resolve conflicts
- Ability to encourage compromise and collaboration
- Emotional competence (i.e., ability to understand others' concerns)
- Focus on unifying seemingly disparate interests of organization and employees
- Patience for pettiness and power plays
- Ability to communicate and persuade stakeholders.

Red-print thinking is focused on getting the most out of the human resources that are required for the change. To incentivize and reward change, leaders must use human resource tools such as rewards, career planning, performance management, recruitment, and selection. As a result, leaders who use red-print thinking will need several competencies:

- Ability to use ethical persuasion and impassioned speechmaking
- Knowledge of, and ability to use, human resource tools (e.g., selection techniques, performance management system, compensation and rewards, and succession planning)
- Patience for differences in employee motivation
- Focus on employees' gifts and talents as they pertain to the desired change
- Attentiveness to working conditions, including security and social issues
- Ability and willingness to model the behavioral changes required
- Ability to listen to employees' concerns and be fully present to them.

Quantum and Dynamic (Continuous) Changes

The final type of change is less prevalent, though it is no less important, than the other three types of changes. It is true that events like mergers and acquisitions usually don't happen every day in most organizations.

But when quantum and dynamic changes occur, they can make or break the organization.

Just like quantum and static change, quantum and dynamic change also rocks people's worlds. The difference is that it goes on for quite a while. Most of the problems with this type of change have to do with the cultural history of the organization: the long-held patterns of behavior, relationships, processes, systems, structures, and values.

For example, many of you may know the saga of General Electric and the National Broadcasting Company (NBC). In 1986, GE acquired NBC, which became a wholly owned subsidiary of GE. The organizations could not have been more dissimilar. GE was a large, conservative, bureaucratic organization that managed largely through systems; NBC had a creative, organic, Hollywood-like culture. In two years, when GE changed the name of the headquarters from the NBC Building to the GE Building, unhappy NBC staffers feared the network was being destroyed and morphed into just another cog in the GE machine. Within another year or two, under the leadership of Jack Welch, the cultural change processes began to work. But it took more than 10 years for the cultural shifts to take hold. Now GE, with its partner Comcast, and NBC together make an entrepreneurial force with good business practices that is in touch with its customers and their needs.

What has to happen during a quantum and dynamic change? First, leaders must recognize that the process cannot be completely structured, because people interact with each other and self-organize somewhat autonomously. Of course, some planned change events are inevitable. But the entire change process cannot be controlled, because organizations are complex and dynamic systems with limited predictability. In other words, during a quantum, dynamic change process, autonomy is the mainstay for ensuring that old patterns of behavior and other obstacles to change are examined and confronted. Therefore, the people, as well as the organization itself, are in a constant change mode, but eventually the system finds its own path and practices that enable lasting changes to occur.

Two approaches to this type of change are appropriate: white-print thinking and green-print thinking. The strengths of the people involved in the change are the driving force behind whether it will be successful and sustainable—in other words, a cultural lens perspective. The necessity for green-print thinking is due to the importance of learning: learning about each other and about the process of, and goals for, the change. Therefore, in addition to the competencies mentioned earlier for green-print thinking, change agents adopting a white-print thinking approach will also need the following capabilities:

- Flexibility and adaptability (in other words, avoidance of rigidity and linear thinking)
- The ability to empower others and avoid micromanaging them
- Innovation and creative energy
- The willingness to let the change process unfold, helping it only when it becomes encumbered with obstacles and barriers that you can help remove
- Ability to live with and encourage healthy conflict
- Facilitation skills
- Focus on the process of the change rather than on the outcome of the change.

Concluding Thoughts

Managers must constantly deal with large and small changes in their organizations. Employees often resist change, primarily because of how it was decided, announced, and implemented. It is incumbent upon all managers to develop the skills and competencies required to bring employees along, as well as getting them motivated to help implement the necessary change.

The majority of you will feel most comfortable and will be most skilled in one of the approaches discussed, just like with the strategic design lens, the political lens, or the cultural lens. However, not all the changes that occur under your leadership will play to your strengths. As a result, you will need to further develop some of the competencies listed under each approach. Many of you may be fairly equal in a couple of the approaches, and that's a good thing!

Now, let's look at the next management role—"Manager as Decisionmaker." In the next chapter we explore some of the reasons organizational decisions are so difficult to make and how you can develop your own decisionmaking competency.

Additional Reading, Resources, and Activities

In order to get the most out of what you've already read, the following are some additional helpful resources and activities.

- Watch the 1987 movie, "Broadcast News" starring William Hurt, Albert Brooks, and Holly Hunter. The television station is going through a major change (downsizing), but the way it is handled causes all kinds of problems for the staff. After watching it, answer these questions:

- - What was the major problem with the way the downsizing and station staffing changes were implemented?

  - What might have helped with communicating the change to staff?

- John Kotter's books *Leading Change* and *The Heart of Change: Real-Life Stories of How People Change Their Organizations* are excellent practical manuals for managers at all levels.

- Think about a significant change in your own life, for example, birth, death, graduation, or a new job, that required new thinking and behaviors on your part. What different skills or competencies did you need to develop in order to make the change successful? What would have helped you prepare for and deal with the subsequent changes required of you?

Manager as Decision-maker and Problem-solver

Sometimes you make the right decision, sometimes you make the decision right.

—Dr. Phil [McGraw], psychologist

There is probably no greater indicator of what managers are all about than the role of decision-maker and problem-solver. We go to managers whenever there are problems that we think require more expertise or experience than we have. We consult with managers when we encounter problems that require multiple stakeholders to weigh in. We count on managers to make decisions that have important consequences for others, i.e., those decisions we consider to be "above our pay grade." In short, we depend on managers to understand the problems in our organizations and to make the hard decisions to solve them.

At its core, *decision-making involves making a choice between at least two alternatives.* However, there are several aspects to making that choice that render decision-making difficult at times: (1) the conditions under which decisions must be made (certainty, risk, uncertainty), (2) our own biases and prejudices (remember schema?), (3) the extent of our responsibility when a decision has consequences for others (ethical dilemmas), and (4) gaining buy-in so that the decision can be implemented expediently and with support from those affected by it. As managers, we routinely face these aspects when we are called upon to make a decision. So, let's look at each of these to see the effects they have on a manager's ability to be a good decision-maker.

Conditions for Decision-making: Certainty, Risk, and Uncertainty

Decisions are made under a variety of conditions. Understanding how the conditions affect the search for alternatives, the assessment of those alternatives, and the ultimate choice among alternatives is crucial to a manager's decision-making process.

A condition of *certainty* exists when the decision-maker knows what the possible alternatives are, the limitations and benefits associated with each alternative, and the likely outcome for each alternative. In essence, certainty suggests that accurate, measurable, and reliable information exists for all possible alternative courses of action, as well as for the consequences of each alternative. With all of this knowledge, a condition of certainty renders the future fairly predictable. Examples of decision-making under conditions of certainty are usually routine and repetitive, such as deciding to comply with a law or regulation or deciding to purchase a machine that can process material most effectively and efficiently.

When managers lack perfect information, or whenever they have information about some (but not all) courses of action, decision risk arises. Under a condition of *risk*, the decision-maker may have some information about available alternatives, but may have only an estimated probability of outcomes for each alternative. That is, there is likely some random variable or unknown source of variation that could affect a decision's actual outcome.

While making decisions under a condition of risk, managers must determine the probability of success associated with each alternative on the basis of the available information and their past experience, if any. The alternative chosen represents a trade-off between the risks and the benefits associated with that particular course of action. An example of a decision made under a condition of risk might be to launch a new product targeted to a known market demographic, but doing so with only an estimate of the probability of making any sales. A good example of this: Coca-Cola's 2004 launch of C2.

For its biggest launch since Diet Coke, Coca-Cola decided that men between 20 and 40 years old who liked the taste of Coke, but who did not like its calories and carbs, would buy their new product, C2, which had half the calories and carbs and all the taste of original Coke. It was introduced in 2004 with a $50 million advertising campaign. However, men rejected the hybrid drink; they wanted full flavor with no calories or carbs, not with half the calories and carbs. The company had some information about what the target demographic wanted, but was not able to estimate with any accuracy whether they would buy the new C2 drink.

Some managers are personally very risk averse, while others don't mind taking a gamble on a decision. It is likely that the specific situation influences them, however. Studies have shown that when the stakes of making an incorrect decision are high, managers are often more averse to taking a risk. Whereas, when the stakes are low, managers are more likely to make a riskier decision.[1]

---

[1] Kahneman, D. and Tversky, A. (1979). Prospect theory: An analysis of decision under risk. *Econometrica*, 47, 263–291.

Finally, many significant managerial decisions are formulated under a state of *uncertainty*. Conditions of uncertainty exist when the future is unpredictable. Moreover, the decision-maker is not aware of all available alternatives, cannot assess all the risks associated with each alternative, or is not sure of the consequences that might result from any particular choice of an alternative. Moreover, even the information that is known may not be completely reliable; therefore, managers have to make assumptions about the situation, depending almost exclusively on judgment and experience.

When we make decisions either under conditions of risk or uncertainty we often rely on past experiences to guide us. While this is helpful in making many decisions, sometimes we rely <u>too</u> heavily on our past experiences, and this can result in biased outcomes.

The Effect of Heuristics and Bias in Decision-making

Recall from our previous discussion of schema in Chapter 1 that all of us bring our personal views of the world to our jobs and that we tend to create mental shortcuts for solving problems and processing information. The technical term for coming up with these "rules of thumb" for making decisions is called *heuristics*. Like schema, they are very helpful for routine decisions, but sometimes in an attempt to simplify our decision-making, heuristics can cause us to oversimplify and ignore pertinent information, thereby reaching an incorrect decision.

Kahneman and his colleagues have spent their careers looking at the effect of reasoning heuristics on decision-making. They have concluded that there are several heuristics that we use frequently, but which can bias our decisions (See Table 2 for a brief summary).[2]

Framing

When we "frame" a problem we are looking at it from a particular point of view, usually whether "gains" or "losses" are emphasized. Consider these two examples of the same problem, albeit framed differently:

> The United States is preparing for an outbreak of a deadly disease. The Center for Disease Control (CDC) is expecting 600 deaths. Two programs can be used to combat the disease. Program A will allow 200 people to be saved. Program B has a 33% probability that all 600 will be saved, and a 67% probability that no one will be saved.

---

[2] See, for example, Tversky, A., & Kahneman, D. (1974). Judgment under uncertainty: Heuristics and biases. *Science, 185*(4157), 1124–1131. doi:10.1126/science.185.4157.1124

Table 2 Examples of Decision-making Heuristics and Potential Biases

Heuristic Name	Heuristic Description	Resulting Bias
Framing	Viewing a problem the way you want to see it	Mistaking your view of the problem for the true problem
Anchoring & Adjustment	Assuming a starting point and thinking about adjustments from there	Being overly dominated by the assumed starting point
Sunk cost	Treating the resources already spent on one alternative as an estimate of the resources you'll have to spend all over again to start a new one.	Treating the resources already spent on one alternative as a real cost of abandoning it for something better
Confirmation	If you're leaning towards an action, you try to prove it's a good one.	If you only look for supporting evidence, you could miss a fatal flaw
Availability	If an idea doesn't fit in with the obvious data, it's surely suspect	Non-obvious things can be most important or most common
Representativeness	"If it looks like a duck and walks like a duck and quacks like a duck, it's probably a duck"	Ignoring the base rate can lead to serious preventable errors

The United States is preparing for an outbreak of a deadly disease. The Center for Disease Control (CDC) is expecting 600 deaths. Two programs can be used to combat the disease. Program A will result in 400 deaths. Program B has a 33% probability that no one will die, and a 67% probability that 600 people will die.

Notice how the first example is "framed" as positive possible outcomes, while the second example is "framed" as negative possible outcomes. The decision to adopt Program A or Program B will depend on the decision-maker seeing the choices as either positive or negative. Usually, decision-makers tend to make less risky decisions when the choices are framed as positive gains (first example) and riskier decisions when the choices are framed negatively as losses, as in the second example.[3]

---

[3] Sitkin, S.B. and Weingart, L.R. (1995). Determinants of risky decision-making behavior: A test of the mediating role of risk perceptions and propensity. *Academy of Management Journal*, 38, 6, 1573–1592.

Anchoring and Adjustment

When we look at a problem and "anchor" the information, we are starting from a hypothetical (and often false) point. For example, many of us have gone to a car lot to trade in our old car and purchase a new one. The car salesman often offers a very low price for our trade-in at the beginning of the negotiations, usually one that is well below the fair market value. Because the salesman "anchored" the starting price at the low price offer, any upward "adjustment" made in our deliberations begins from that unreasonably low price. Then, when the salesman finally offers what we consider a reasonable price, we will tend to accept it, thinking that we have managed to get him to go higher and, therefore, we have come out ahead.

In management we often are presented with "best case" or "worst case" scenarios. Both of these extremes serve as starting anchors for our decision. Consider a case where we must decide whether to introduce a new product under a "best case" scenario in which there will be few competing products. Under the anchoring and adjustment heuristic, we will tend to overestimate how well our product will do. Under highly competitive conditions where there could be many competitors ("worst case"), we will be likely to underestimate the success of our product.

Sunk Costs

Making a decision based on thinking about how much we have already invested in the decision is known as "sunk costs." In this heuristic, we decide to continue on with a course of action, even when it makes no practical sense to do so. Sticking with our used car example for the moment, if you had to pour money into that old car just to keep it going, you might have thought, "Well, I've already spent $800 on this car, so I might as well keep it a bit longer, rather than trade it in." If, however, in two months you end up spending another $300, you've made the "sunk cost" decision even worse!

Our sunk cost bias can send us into a vicious cycle of increasing our commitments to a decision. Psychologists call this *escalation of commitment*, and research has found that our decisions are affected by how much we have invested already and by whether our decision choice is framed as a gain (i.e., not risking any more of our resources) or as a loss (i.e., having risked a lot of our resources already).[4,5] One of the major downsides to escalation in our commitment to a decision is that we tend to get very defensive and refuse to

[4] Bazerman, M.H. (1986). *Judgment in managerial decision making*. New York: Wiley.
[5] Schoorman, F.D., Mayer, R.C., Douglas, C.A., and Hetrick, C.T. (1994). Escalation of commitment and the framing effect: An empirical investigation. *Journal of Applied Social Psychology*, 24, 6, 509–528.

change our minds, even in the face of evidence that suggests we should abandon the decision we made. In some cases we become even more committed to it the more invested we become. A good example of this is gambling. The more chronic gamblers lose, the more they try to recoup their losses by betting even more money.

Confirmation

People with strong beliefs have a greater tendency to look for information to confirm what they already think. This is particularly true for value-based beliefs that are deeply entrenched (e.g., death penalty, gun rights, abortion, affirmative action, legalization of marijuana, global warming ... the list is endless). To test this hypothesis, a team at Stanford University conducted an experiment involving participants who felt strongly about capital punishment, with half in favor of it and half against it.[6] Each participant read descriptions of two studies. The first was a comparison of U.S. states that had or did not have the death penalty. The second looked at a comparison of murder rates in a state before and after the introduction of the death penalty. After reading a detailed account of each study's procedure, they rated whether the research was well-conducted and convincing. Half the participants were told that one kind of study supported the deterrent effect and the other undermined it, while for the other half those conclusions were reversed.

Almost all the participants, whether initial supporters or opponents of the death penalty, returned to their original belief regardless of the evidence provided in the studies they read, pointing to details that supported their initial viewpoint and disregarding anything that was contrary to it. The major conclusion of the study was that people set higher standards of evidence for hypotheses that go against their current beliefs.

Confirmation bias can be seen most starkly in organizations when managers need to change a process, adopt a new approach, or consider a policy that conflicts with their values or beliefs. The more staunchly held the value or belief, the more difficult it becomes for managers to decide to enact the new process, approach, or policy.

Availability

One of the most common biases we all have is based on how easily we can call to mind information related to the frequency or importance of events. When

---

[6] Lord, C.G., Ross, L., and Lepper, M.R. (1979). Biased assimilation and attitude polarization: The effects of prior theories on subsequently considered evidence, *Journal of Personality and Social Psychology*, American Psychological Association, 37, 11, 2098–209.

trying to make a decision, a number of related events or situations might immediately come to mind, e.g., how likely is it that a school shooting will occur in my child's school? As a result, we tend to give greater credence to this information and tend to overestimate the probability and likelihood of similar things happening in the future. This is referred to as the availability heuristic.

Tversky and Kahneman (1974) reported a study in which participants were read a list of the names of well-known male and female celebrities and asked to say whether, overall, more men or more women were on the list. In one group, the list contained more famous women than men, but actually had more men's names on the list. In the second group, the list had more famous men than women, but had a greater number of women's names overall. In both cases, the participants incorrectly guessed that the sex with more famous names also had the higher number. The ease of recall of the famous names, i.e., the "availability" of the information to the participants, led them to the false conclusion.

Overall, the availability heuristic merely means that people are prone to believe what they want to believe, and it is uncomfortable and counterintuitive to search for evidence that contradicts our beliefs. In management, we see this play out in multiple ways. For example, when we interview candidates, we tend to recall previous successful or unsuccessful employees who went to a particular university and erroneously predict that others who went to that university will behave similarly. Sometimes, managers lack the time or resources to investigate possible alternatives in greater depth. Faced with the need for an immediate decision, the availability heuristic allows them to quickly arrive at a conclusion.

Representativeness

Sometimes we may be likely to make more errors in our decisions because we overestimate the likelihood that something will occur. This happens because we associate an event, person, or object with certain characteristics that we think are "representative" of the event or object. But just because something is representative does not mean its occurrence is more probable. Likewise, decisions that are based on the representativeness heuristic can lead to prejudice, stereotyping, and discriminatory decision-making.

Tversky and Kahneman describe one example of how the representativeness heuristic can influence our perceptions of other people.[7] They describe an individual [Steve] who is seen as shy, withdrawn, and helpful. This person is also described as tidy, meek, and detailed with a passion for order and

[7] Tversky, A., & Kahneman, D. (1974). Judgment under uncertainty: Heuristics and biases. *Science, 185*(4157), 1124–1131. doi:10.1126/science.185.4157.1124

structure. When participants were asked about which profession Steve likely holds—farmer, salesman, airline pilot, librarian, or physician—the majority said that Steve was a librarian. Their decision was based on the degree to which the characteristics that described Steve were representative of, or similar to, the stereotype they held of a librarian.

While the "Steve" example is fairly innocuous, when managers judge all classes of people (race, sex, gender, marital status, religious affiliation, different abilities, etc.), their decisions are likely to have discriminatory effects.

We are all affected by this bias, particularly in advertising where companies use representativeness to convince us that products are representative of a trait we might have or our idealized self. For example, a suave man drinking a certain beverage and who is surrounded by beautiful women leads us to believe that by drinking that beverage we are more likely to be suave and interesting, too.

Overall, we use reasoning heuristics to help us make decisions more quickly and efficiently. However, we must be cautious as managers not to rely solely on these short cuts, but to search out information that can challenge our beliefs, disconfirm our prior hypotheses, and generally provide us with a valid and reliable basis for our decisions.

Group Decision-making Biases

As a manager, it is likely that you will call upon others to give you input into your decisions or, occasionally, to make a decision as a group. In addition to the individual-level biases already discussed, there are some interesting aspects to involving others in a decision-making process, and we will discuss two of the more common ones: failure to manage conflict and failure to manage agreement.

Failure to Manage Conflict: The Case of the Challenger Disaster

On Jan. 28, 1986, the space shuttle Challenger broke apart 73 seconds after launch. The crew quickly lost consciousness from air loss after the breakup. They died about three minutes later, when the cabin hit the Atlantic Ocean.

Why did this happen?

Sadly, it occurred because of several reasons, not the least of which was the inability to manage conflict between the shuttle's design engineers at Morton Thiokol and the NASA managers of the Marshall Space Flight Center regarding the decision to launch the Challenger under extremely low air temperature. Let's look at some things that influenced the failure to manage the conflict and the decision biases surrounding what has come to be called the Challenger Disaster.

One major influence was that NASA had a long history of success that included the Apollo missions to the moon and the Skylab space station project. While some glitches had occurred over the years (such as the Apollo 13 in-flight emergency in 1970), the glitches were never large enough to be destructive to human life. The shuttle missions prior to Challenger had accomplished various activities: they launched satellites, repaired them in orbit, and recovered and returned them to Earth. This latter activity saved NASA a tremendous amount of money, too.

Their previous successes were interpreted to mean that because they had been successful in the past, they would be successful in the future, and this created excessive optimism. When groups believe that they will be successful in the future because of past successes, they tend to ignore obvious dangers and make riskier decisions.[8] This is known as an *illusion of invulnerability.*

A second influence was that NASA managers and the engineers at Morton Thiokol (the contracted manufacturer) had been aware of problems with joints of the solid rocket booster and the O-ring seals since 1977, but they never considered them a real threat. The engineers at Thiokol discovered a problem known as "joint rotation," during tests in 1977. However, Thiokol engineers did not believe that joint rotation would cause significant problems, but when they reported it to NASA engineers at The Marshall Space Flight Center, they thought just the opposite. Marshall's engineers recommended a redesign of the joint and had some specific modifications in mind. However, Thiokol did not consider a redesign necessary. Continual problems related to the O-rings were found over the next several years. In 1985 they discovered that as the temperature was lowered, the O-rings lost resilience and the ability to function at all. In fact, they noticed that the O-rings' erosion allowed hot gases to blow back, causing the potential for an explosion. Concerned that the blowback, combined with the erosion problem, might lead to grave consequences, Roger Boisjoly, a Thiokol engineer, wrote to his Vice President of Engineering, Robert Lund, in July, 1985,

> ... It is my honest and very real fear that if we do not take immediate action to dedicate a team to solve the problem, with the field joint having the number one priority, then we stand in jeopardy of losing a flight with all the launch pad facilities ....

Although both NASA and Thiokol's management team first failed to recognize it as a problem, then failed to fix it, and finally treated it as an acceptable flight risk, NASA and Thiokol managers proceeded with the launch on January 28, 1986 despite strong appeals from Thiokol engineers not to do so. Engineers at Thiokol appealed to managers at Thiokol and NASA

---

[8] Janis, I.L. (1972). *Victims of Groupthink.* New York: Houghton Mifflin.

on the evening of January 27th to delay the launch, because they were highly concerned about potential O-ring malfunction, primarily because the ambient temperatures predicted for launch day were much lower than what earlier launches had ever experienced. The Thiokol managers and the NASA managers then had a private five-minute meeting (although it was in the presence of the engineers who were not polled for their opinions), during which they decided to launch the next day anyway, despite the low temperature. As we now know, that decision ended in total disaster.

The group of managers engaged in *collective rationalization*, in which group members discount warnings about the information they receive, and the engineers experienced *pressure on dissenters*, in which those opposed are under pressure not to offer dissenting opinions that run counter to the group's views (in this case, the views of the group of managers). All of these influences, plus several more, are part of a larger phenomenon known as *groupthink*.

Groupthink, a term coined by social psychologist Irving Janis in 1972, occurs when a group makes faulty decisions because of group pressures. These pressures, in turn, lead to a deterioration of "mental efficiency, reality testing, and moral judgment."[9] Groups affected by groupthink tend to make irrational decisions and reach consensus prematurely on what they should do or which decision they should make. A group is especially vulnerable to groupthink when its members are similar in background, when the group is insulated from outside opinions, and when there are no clear rules for decision making.[10] Janis documented eight symptoms of groupthink:[11]

1. *Illusion of Invulnerability*: Ignoring obvious danger and taking extreme risk
2. *Collective Rationalization*: Explaining away contrary warnings
3. *Illusion of Morality*: Ignoring the ethical consequences of decisions
4. *Excessive Stereotyping*: Constructing negative stereotypes of rivals
5. *Pressure for Conformity*: Pressuring any member in the group to conform
6. *Self-Censorship*: Withholding dissenting views
7. *Illusion of Unanimity*: Perceiving (falsely) that everyone agrees with the group's decision
8. *Mindguards*: Protecting the group from adverse information that might threaten group complacency

---

[9] Janis, I. L. (1972). *Victims of Groupthink*. New York: Houghton Mifflin, p.9.
[10] Ibid.
[11] Janis, I.L., & Mann, L. (1977). Decision making: A psychological analysis of conflict, choice and commitment. New York: Macmillan.

In order to overcome a groupthink tendency, some experts believe that group leaders and facilitators should adopt the following practices:

- Make the group aware of the causes and consequences of groupthink.
- The leader should withhold all preferences and expectations until the end of discussion.
- The leader should encourage objections and doubts, as well as accept criticism.
- Assign the role of devil's advocate to a member of the group.
- Break the group up to deliberate or include expert opinions from outside.
- Spend time surveying all warning signals from rival group or organizations.
- Tentative decisions should be discussed with trusted colleagues not in the decision-making group.

Although leaders have a role in mitigating groupthink through better managing conflict, they often face another kind of management challenge when making decisions as a group—the failure to manage agreement.

Failure to Manage Agreement: The Case of The Abilene Paradox

It does sound strange that managing agreement would be difficult. But sometimes that is exactly what we face as managers when we have to make decisions that involve others. In a group setting the mismanagement of agreement occurs when members publicly voice their support for an idea or decision, but they privately disagree with it. The classic example of this phenomenon is known as "The Abilene Paradox."

Jerry Harvey was a young, assistant professor of management when he made a serendipitous discovery about the power of contradiction in organizations in a very unlikely place—Abilene, Texas. While he and his wife were visiting her parents in Coleman, Texas one very hot, dusty week, his father-in-law suddenly suggested that all four of them go to Abilene for dinner at the cafeteria. Jerry recounts the trip:[12]

> I thought, "What, go to Abilene? Fifty-three miles? In this dust storm and heat? And in an unairconditioned 1958 Buick?"
>
> But my wife chimed in with, "Sounds like a great idea. I'd like to go. How about you, Jerry?"

---

[12] Harvey, J. B. (1974). The Abilene paradox: the management of agreement. *Organizational Dynamics*, 3, 63–80.

Since my own preferences were obviously out of step with the rest I replied, "Sounds good to me," and added, "I just hope your mother wants to go."

"Of course I want to go," said my mother-in-law. "I haven't been to Abilene in a long time."

So into the car and off to Abilene we went. My predictions were fulfilled. The heat was brutal. We were coated with a fine layer of dust that was cemented with perspiration by the time we arrived. The food at the cafeteria provided first-rate testimonial material for antacid commercials. Some four hours and 106 miles later we returned to Coleman, hot and exhausted. We sat in front of the fan for a long time in silence.

Then, both to be sociable and to break the silence, I said, "It was a great trip, wasn't it?"

No one spoke. Finally my mother-in-law said, with some irritation, "Well, to tell the truth, I really didn't enjoy it much and would rather have stayed here. I just went along because the three of you were so enthusiastic about going. I wouldn't have gone if you all hadn't pressured me into it."

I couldn't believe it. "What do you mean 'you all'?" I said. "Don't put me in the 'you all' group. I was delighted to be doing what we were doing. I didn't want to go. I only went to satisfy the rest of you. You're the culprits."

My wife looked shocked. "Don't call me a culprit. You and Daddy and Mama were the ones who wanted to go. I just went along to be sociable and to keep you happy. I would have had to be crazy to want to go out in heat like that."

Her father entered the conversation abruptly. "Hell!" he said. He proceeded to expand on what was already absolutely clear. "Listen, 1 never wanted to go to Abilene. I just thought you might be bored. You visit so seldom I wanted to be sure you enjoyed it. I would have preferred to play another game of dominoes and eat the leftovers in the icebox."

The question is, of course, why did they go? As he thought about that question, Harvey came to realize that organizations often take similar trips that they really don't want to take. In fact, he describes how The Abilene Paradox works to derail organizational decision-making:

> Organizations frequently take actions in contradiction to what they really want to do and therefore defeat the very purposes they are trying to achieve. It also deals with a major corollary of the paradox, which is that the inability to manage agreement is a major source of organization dysfunction ....

it is my contention that the inability to cope with (manage) agreement, rather than the inability to cope with (manage) conflict, is the single most pressing issue of modern organizations.

The causes of the paradox are based to a large degree on the failure to communicate one's desires to everyone else in the group, but this failure is based largely on fear and anxiety about being branded as "not a team player," or being ostracized from the group. In essence, having anxiety about losing others' approval is a huge motivation for not speaking one's mind and, consequently, not achieving the desired goals for the organization. As a manager, being able to take the risks required to question assumptions, search for facts, assert one's opinion, and make the decision takes courage. But it is the only way to appear credible and trustworthy in your role as a decision-maker.

Gaining Buy-in for Decisions

The ultimate goal of managerial decision-making is gaining buy-in for the decisions you make so that they can be correctly implemented. There are three ways to do this: by compliance, by agreement, or by consensus.

In compliance, the participants agree to abide by the decision, primarily because there is some adverse consequence if they don't. For example, we comply with a traffic law ("No U-Turn) so that we avoid getting a ticket, even if we find it inconvenient to drive another block or two. Compliance from a manager's point of view is not a long-term strategy, but a means of getting people to do something in the moment by exerting power to reward or punish them. It is really a decision that has already been made, and the strategy is to get whatever has been decided under way.

In agreement, everyone actually works on the details of the decision until a substantial majority of all concerned agree that it is the right decision or, at least, the most expedient one. This is often achieved by voting and is often difficult to achieve in a diverse group unless one is a very skilled facilitator.

Consensus is different from both compliance and agreement. Instead of simply voting for an item and having the majority of the group "win," a group using consensus is committed to finding solutions that everyone actively supports or, at least, can live with. Consensus also helps insure that all opinions and concerns have been taken into account.

Resolving Ethical Dilemmas in Decision-making

Most people in organizations—and especially managers—will be confronted frequently with having to make decisions that have no clear right or wrong answer. This is particularly true with decisions that involve ethical questions in which the decision-maker faces an *ethical dilemma*. At its core, an ethical dilemma involves three conditions:

1. There must be a choice between at least two options in which each has an ethical standard, but each of the standards are in conflict with the other.
2. There must be consequences of the decision for someone other than the decision-maker.
3. The decision-maker is accountable for the consequences occurring because of the decision s/he makes.

For example, Kidder has identified several of these dilemmas that we face every day in organizations:[13]

- Truth vs loyalty
- Individual vs community
- Short-term vs long-term
- Justice vs mercy

These decision dilemmas ultimately involve a balancing act between our choices. For example, managers often are forced to choose between a decision that achieves short-term gains or one that has short-term losses, but achieves long-term gains. Governments are sometimes faced with balancing the rights of individual citizens with the good of the overall community. Employees experiencing harassing behavior from their managers have to balance the consequences of a decision that brings out the truth, but that ruins the personal or professional lives of those involved.

The real difficulty of an ethical dilemma is that reasonable people disagree about what is "right," "just," or "fair." In other words, each of us has our own view on what we consider to be "ethical." As a manager, it is helpful to understand some different models of ethical viewpoints, not only because it helps you to make these complex decisions, but also because, by doing so, you can understand why other people may see the situation differently.

There are basically three major approaches to making a decision on an ethical issue in organizations:

- *The Utilitarian Approach* emphasizes the "Results" of a decision. In this approach it is considered an ethical action if it provides the most good

---

[13] Kidder, RM. (1995). *How good people make tough choices: Resolving the dilemmas of ethical living.* New York, NY: Simon and Schuster.

or does the least harm for the greatest number of stakeholders affected—e.g., customers, employees, shareholders, the community, and the environment.

- *The Deontological Approach* emphasizes the "Rights" involved in a decision. This approach starts from the belief that humans have an ability and a right to choose freely what they do with their lives. In essence, people have the right to make their own choices, to be told the truth, to avoid injury, to a degree of privacy, and so on. People who adopt this ethical approach to decision-making see an action as ethical if it is the one that best protects and respects the rights of those affected.
- *The Distributive Justice Approach* considers the "Relationship" between the positive and negative outcomes of a decision. People who use this approach see actions as ethical if they treat all human beings equally or, at least, equitably based on some standard that is defensible. In essence, the approach says that one stakeholder should not shoulder all the burdens of a decision while another stakeholder gets all the blessings of it; rather, to be considered ethical, the "blessings and burdens" of a decision should be shared as equally as possible among stakeholders.

Once we understand our own preferred way of "seeing" an ethical dilemma, and we can interpret how people who may disagree with us view it, we can better understand why they are opposed. Our preferred ethical lens has developed over our lifetimes, so it takes some effort on our part to recognize that others do not see things the same way that we do. And, like much of what we have already discussed so far, it also takes effort on our part to try to see things from a different lens ourselves. Once we can do that, we have a chance to incorporate divergent viewpoints as we attempt to resolve our dilemma through our decision-making process.

Using an Ethical Decision-making Process

In addition to knowing HOW we see an ethical dilemma, it is also important to have a process for resolving it. The following is one suggested approach that has elements that allow us to understand and evaluate ethical issues that may be embedded in our decision.

First, we need to know the facts surrounding our decision, i.e., under which conditions we are making the decision, what information we already know about the aspects of the decision, timelines for the decision, etc.

Next comes the consideration of any ethical issues that may be present. This is also the spot to identify conflicts in ethical views and standards, questions that have arisen or may arise about the fairness of the decision, or the ethics of the decision process itself.

Third, we want to identify the primary stakeholders in the decision. These stakeholders include anyone who would be affected by our decision, such as customers, employees, vendors, the community-at-large, or others. As the "Rights" approach suggests, these folks have the right to be consulted before actually making the final decision.

At this point we want to begin to identify possible alternatives for our decision and, most importantly, we want to evaluate the ethics of those alternatives, as well as the practical implications of each alternative, i.e., to determine if we can actually implement the decision with the resources we have. Finally, after evaluation—both ethical and practical—we are ready to make our decision.

Concluding Thoughts

It has probably become obvious that there is much more to a manager's role of decision-maker than meets the eye. Not only do managers need to understand whether the decision is made under conditions of risk or uncertainty, but they also need to be able to identify and monitor their own potential perceptual biases, get buy-in for their decisions, and make sure that they are able to recognize when a decision has ethical implications for others. In the next chapter we look at another important managerial role: "Manager as Motivator and Encourager."

Additional Reading, Resources, and Activities

In order to get the most out of what you've already read, the following are some additional helpful resources and activities.

- When have you had a disagreement with someone that you now see was because of differences in your preferred ethical lens and theirs? How did you resolve it then, and how might you resolve it now, knowing what you now know about different ethical perspectives?

- Try using the Ethical Decision-making Process outlined in this chapter to see how it might work with this hypothetical case:

  - Lorna is an administrative assistant in the Human Resources Department. Her good friend, Bill, is applying for a job with the company, and she has agreed to serve as a reference for him. Bill approaches her for advice on preparing for the interview. Lorna has the actual interview questions asked of all applicants and considers making him a copy of the list so he can adequately prepare. Using the ethical decision-making process, what would each of the three approaches (Results, Rights, Relationship) suggest she do?

- **Arthur Andersen Case Studies in Business Ethics**

  Practice cases. During the period 1987–94 Arthur Andersen funded a $5 million joint project with 525 universities to raise awareness of ethical issues in business. This collection of 90 case studies is one product of that effort. All universities have license to use these materials and reproduce them as needed for instructional purposes. http://public.tepper.cmu.edu/ethics/aa/arthurandersen.htm

Manager as Motivator and Encourager

Whether you think you can or you think you can't, you're right.

—Henry Ford

One of the most frustrating things for managers is to have direct reports who appear to be disengaged from their jobs. The symptoms of disengagement often look like these:

- They don't seem interested in learning new things.
- They may avoid volunteering to help others.
- They often "disappear" during a very busy time.
- They may not be performing as well as they once did.
- They may withdraw psychologically from their peers and manager.
- They may start missing work a lot or calling in sick when they really aren't.

Astute managers notice this disengagement and try to "fix" it. Sometimes they try something vague, such as "if you ever need to talk, my door is always open." Unfortunately, the employee usually doesn't pick up on such subtlety. Sometimes managers assume what the problem is without actually verifying it ("she's looking for another job that pays more money"), and then jump to a solution that they think solves the problem ("we are promoting you").

Of course, neither of these approaches works, primarily because most managers really don't know the fundamental causes of disengagement. In fact, in most organizations the question of *why* employees become disengaged often remains a complete mystery. There are myriad reasons why someone is disengaged and not motivated to come to work or to do their work, and we will look at just a few of them in a moment. First, however, let's be clear what we mean by "motivation."

What is "Motivation"?

There are several ways motivation has been defined and studied, but for our purposes here we will use this definition: **Motivation is an internal cognitive**

process that describes the level, direction, and persistence of effort that one expends toward some end. Notice the words "internal" and "cognitive" here. They imply that motivation originates inside someone and that it is an intentional decision process. Interestingly, this definition also points to the fact that an individual employee cannot be "motivated" by someone else, e.g., a manager. Rather, this process occurs within the employee.

Why is this so important for a manager to know?

Primarily, because *managers don't motivate anyone to do anything*! Employees motivate themselves. But, that doesn't mean that managers don't have a role to play in employee motivation and engagement. In fact, their role is crucial in creating the environment so that employees intentionally decide how much and which type of effort they want to expend doing their work and developing their relationships in the organization.

It is highly unlikely that new employees begin their new jobs unmotivated and disengaged. Instead, we could reasonably assume that they become unmotivated and disengaged after they join their organizations, which means that managers, the culture and systems of the company, their peers, or any number of things cause their disengagement and decision to reduce their efforts.

When employees decide to disengage, they usually have some very good reasons. In order to understand why employees may decide they don't wish to expend effort, let's begin by looking at some of the specific reasons for employee disengagement.

Reasons for Employee Disengagement

Reason #1: I don't like the work I do. Of course, this makes all the sense in the world: if you don't like what you're doing, you will try to avoid doing it whenever you can. Who wants to spend their days doing things they hate?

Keep in mind that in any job we have to do certain tasks that we don't really like, but we usually have things in our jobs that we do like. For disengaged employees it may be that they are required to spend a larger percentage of their time on those things they don't like than on the things they do like. Naturally, the more tasks they have that they don't like, the more disengaged and de-motivated they will become. However, it is possible to help employees reframe the importance and value of their tasks and job, even in jobs in which the work itself is not the most pleasant.

Martin Seligman has a wonderful story in his book, *Authentic Happiness*.[1] He recounts visiting a good friend in the hospital and being present when an

---

[1] Seligman, M. E. P. (2002). *Authentic happiness: Using the new positive psychology to realize your potential for lasting fulfillment*. New York: Free Press.

orderly came into the room. The man proceeded to take out pictures from his bag and fix them to the wall, just beyond the foot of the patient's bed. Seligman asked him what he was doing.

"I'm an orderly on this floor," he answered. "But I bring in new prints and photos every week. You see, I'm responsible for the health of all these patients. Take Mr. Miller here. He hasn't woken up since they brought him in, but when he does, I want to make sure he sees beautiful things right away."

This hospital orderly, concludes Seligman, "did not define his work as the emptying of bedpans or the swabbing of trays, but as protecting the health of his patients and procuring objects to fill this difficult time of their lives with beauty. He may have held a lowly job, but he crafted it into a high calling."

Managers who can help employees reframe their jobs or tasks as having value to customers, patients, other employees, or the overall organization create more engagement opportunities. And the more opportunities there are for employees to engage with their jobs, the more individual motivation will increase.

Reason #2: I don't feel like I "fit" with this job. Even if an employee likes his job, he may still not feel that it is a good fit for his skills. One of the areas that managers have quite a bit of influence on is making sure that the skill level of employees matches the difficulty and complexity required by the tasks. For example, if employees with low skill levels are put into difficult or complex jobs, they will experience anxiety and stress, primarily because they don't feel capable of performing well. Additionally, there have been a number of research studies on why an employee perceives his job as stressful, including those that compare the quantity and quality of the demands of the job (pacing or workload) with the amount of control an employee feels she has over those demands.[2] We also know that conflict (such as role conflict or family-work conflict)[3] or time-related challenges (work deadlines or long commutes)[4] tend to create a stressful work environment. Overall, when employees feel that the job requirements exceed their ability to perform at their best, they become de-motivated.

---

[2] See, for example, Fox, M. L., Dwyer, D. J., & Ganster, D. C. (1993). Effects of stressful job demands and control on physiological and attitudinal outcomes in a hospital setting. *Academy of Management Journal, 36*, 2, 289–318.

[3] Frone, M.R., Russell, M., & Cooper, M.L. (1992). Antecedents and outcomes of work-family conflict: A model of the work-family interface. *Journal of Applied Psychology, 77*, 65–78.

[4] Voydanoff, P. (2005). Consequences of boundary-spanning demands and resources for work-to-family conflict and perceived stress. *Journal of Occupational Health Psychology, 10*, 4, 491–503.

Likewise, poor job fit can also occur when employees who have relatively high skills are assigned menial tasks. In this case, these employees will get bored. Sometimes bored employees try to keep motivated by creating games or competitions with others or themselves, e.g., "I'll race you to see who can stock these shelves the fastest. Ready ... Go!" In most cases, however, these games eventually get old, and when they do, disengagement occurs.[5] Whether employees are experiencing anxiety and stress or just plain boredom, employees who are in jobs in which their skills levels and task requirements don't match will give up putting in effort, become disengaged, and ultimately get fired or quit.

But managers can avoid either of these scenarios by making sure that candidates are fully aware of the job requirements during initial interviews. Using realistic job previews, job podcasts, and talking with employees currently in the job under consideration can help people decide whether they want to continue on in the process. It is always better to have employees self-select themselves out of the process early on than it is to have them start the job and then quit or be terminated because of poor job-person fit.

It is also possible that managers are looking in the wrong places for their employees. For example, some low skill tasks may not require high school diplomas or even stellar references. The search for more employees willing to do menial tasks is increasingly troubling many employers.[6] But looking at different populations, such as ex-felons and differently-abled individuals, may provide a fresh pool of candidates whose skills better match the job requirements. The bottom line is that matching skill levels with the tasks required cannot be overstated in stemming some employees' reasons for becoming disengaged and de-motivated.

Reason #3: I don't feel like I "fit" in this organization. We have already addressed the issue of organizational culture and how important it is to have shared values, assumptions, stories, rituals, celebrations, and norms. If an employee doesn't share in those things, at least to some degree, he or she will likely decide to disengage, either mentally or physically, and may decide to leave the organization all together at some point. Moreover, disengaged employees often become ostracized because they don't "fit in" with the rest

---

[5] Harju, L.K. and Hakanen, J.J. (2016). An employee who was not there: a study of job boredom in white-collar work, *Personnel Review*, 45, 2, 374–391. https://doi.org/10.1108/PR-05-2015-0125

[6] Maxwell, Nan L. (2006). Low-skilled jobs: The reality behind the popular perceptions. In *The Working Life: The Labor Market for Workers in Low-Skilled Jobs*. Kalamazoo, MI: W.E. Upjohn Institute for Employment Research, 1–23. https://doi.org/10.17848/ 9781429454902

of the team, sometimes resulting in deviant behavior,[7] e.g., sabotaging their own work or the work of those who have ostracized them, employee theft, or verbal abuse. In a worst-case scenario, they may even turn to workplace violence.

It behooves managers to discover as soon as possible those employees who are having trouble fitting into the culture of the department or the organization. Learn to recognize signs of cultural disengagement, like the following examples, so that you might intervene earlier, rather than waiting until the employee is completely disengaged:

- Employee doesn't attend celebrations or social gatherings with peers.
- Employee frequently violates unwritten social norms (e.g., dress code, social media usage, excessive break times) or written policies (e.g., attendance, tardiness).
- Employee avoids interacting with other employees unless s/he absolutely has to as a part of a task.
- Employee doesn't contribute ideas or suggestions voluntarily or when asked.

The reality of cultural misfit is that employees will not necessarily leave the organization unless and until it gets so uncomfortable that they feel they can't stay. As a manager, if you recognize that employees cannot or will not adapt to your organization's culture, it is in both the employees' and the organization's best interests not to belittle them, ignore them, or ostracize them, but to help them find another place to work.

Reason #4: I don't feel valued by the organization or my manager. This is an all-too-common complaint by a lot of employees. A chronic feeling of being undervalued for their skills and expertise has a tendency to eventually affect an employee's self-esteem and personal value. It also results in increasing disengagement: "They don't appreciate me, so why am I putting in all this effort?"

Employees may feel unappreciated when they are not able to use their full skills and talents in their job, when their future potential is never mentioned, when their hard work or effort is not recognized, or when they don't see the organization willing to invest in them with more training or development opportunities. Whether managers believe these perceptions to be true or not, they need to know that the feeling of not being appreciated or valued is real for many employees.

---

[7] Robinson, S.L. and Bennett, R.J. (1995). A typology of deviant workplace behaviors: A multidimensional scaling study. *The Academy of Management Journal*, 38, 2, 555–572.

The great thing is that conveying value and appreciation to your employees is free! As a manager, it is within your power every day to make sure that your employees feel appreciated and valued. In doing so, you will be able to create a culture of appreciation that goes a long way toward stemming employee disengagement.

Reason #5: I don't like, respect, or trust my boss. This is a tough one, but it is one of the main reasons for employee disengagement.[8] You'll remember from Chapter 5 that trustworthiness is a key element for managers. If employees don't trust their managers or senior leaders, it is just a matter of time before they become disengaged and eventually leave the organization. Moreover, employees who don't trust their bosses tell others about their experiences, so this trust issue follows those managers around wherever they go.

But there is no requirement that your employees like you—it helps, but it isn't required. In fact, if more than 70% of your employees actually like you, then you may not be making the hard decisions, evaluating their work honestly, or challenging them enough so that they grow and develop. If it is important to you that your employees like you, then management may be the wrong profession for you!

Having said that, there are some things that promote employees' respect for their managers. First, a manager can never communicate expectations too much. Employees should always know what is expected of them and should always know where they stand. They should never be surprised if you tell them they are under-performing, because a good manager constantly provides feedback and guidance. Additionally, listen to what they are saying about their challenges and issues, and then offer assistance. One of the best questions to ask them is, "how can I be helpful?" It may be that they can't think of any way you can be helpful at that moment, but the mere fact that you've asked them is appreciated.

Second, always be respectful to your employees. It is hard to expect people to respect you if you don't respect them. Avoid yelling or belittling anyone. No one likes or respects a boss who is a bully.

Finally, always give your employees credit for the things that go well, and take the blame for things that fail. Try to be constantly on the lookout for opportunities for your employees to shine, grow, and be in the spotlight. When you do, your employees will feel more appreciated, be willing to go above and beyond, and ultimately feel more engaged.

---

[8] Branham, L. (2012). *The 7 hidden reasons why employees leave: How to recognize the subtle signs and act before it's too late.* New York: AMACOM.

The bottom line is that managers should not be looking for ways to make people happy; rather, should be looking for ways to stop them from being unhappy. Addressing the things that cause disengagement won't immediately lead to engaged employees, but it will make employees feel less disengaged and get them pointed in a more positive and productive direction. It is an effective manager who can recognize, too, that there will be some employees who will not ever engage or be motivated where they currently work, and that means helping them to find another place to work where they can be motivated and engaged. It is what trustworthy managers do.

Using Psychology to Create More Employee Engagement

Now that we know some of the things that cause employees to become disengaged and de-motivated, it is now time to focus on creating a more motivating, engaging environment for employees. To begin, it would be helpful to look at the role of self-fulfilling prophecy and its influence on employee motivation.

Self-fulfilling Prophecy: The Effect of Positive and Negative Expectations

In psychology there is a preponderance of evidence that our beliefs and expectations influence outcomes and behaviors, even when we are not aware that we even hold those expectations. One example of this is what is generally known as the *placebo effect*, first discovered during clinical trials of treatments for diseases.[9] In essence, it is found when one group of participants is given the actual medicinal treatment under investigation, while the other group is given a treatment that has no medicinal effects. The placebo effect refers to the improvements in outcomes that are caused by the participants' belief in the effectiveness of the "treatment" they received, even though they did not receive any medicinal treatment at all. This effect has proven to be so powerful that virtually all clinical trials now control for a placebo effect.

One variation of the placebo effect in educational and organizational settings has come to be known as the *Pygmalion Effect*, so named because of Ovid's Greek legend of the Cypriot sculptor, Pygmalion. The story goes that after searching high and low for the perfect woman, he decided that she did not exist and set about carving an ivory statue of a woman he believed had all

---

[9] Kaptchuk, T.J. (1998). Powerful placebo: the dark side of the randomised controlled trial. *Lancet,* 351,1722–1725. doi: 10.1016/S0140-6736(97)10111–8.

the attributes he desired. When he finished, he immediately fell in love with the statue. He prayed to Aphrodite, the goddess of love, to bring him a woman in the likeness of the statue. When he returned home he found that Aphrodite had brought the actual statue to life, and they got married.

In educational settings the Pygmalion Effect is often found when teachers let their students know that they believe in their ability to succeed in a test or to achieve certain grades. In management, the Pygmalion Effect can be seen in those expectations we hold about our subordinates and direct reports. It works something like this:

1. Managers have expectations of and for their subordinates.
2. Managers convey their expectations to employees consciously (e.g., verbally and in writing) and unconsciously (e.g., body language, expressions, and vocal tone).
3. Subordinates receive and interpret the message of what is expected of them.
4. Subordinates strive to perform and live up to the expectations of their manager.
5. When they live up to those expectations, they reinforce their managers' beliefs.

Another variation is known as the *Galatea Effect* (which, interestingly, was the name of Pygmalion's statue-wife). This is when employees' own opinions about their abilities and self-worth influence their performance. You'll notice that this differs slightly from the Pygmalion Effect because it is self-driven, i.e., if employees think they can perform well, they will; if they think they can't perform well, they won't. Of course, the best of both worlds is when both the employees and their managers have confidence in their performance.

The opposite result can also be true, of course, and this is often referred to as the *Golem Effect*. According to 16th century Jewish folklore, a rabbi from Prague created a golem from clay to protect the city from the impending plague. Unfortunately, the golem became corrupt and went about destroying the city instead of protecting it. Eventually, the golem was destroyed by its creator in order to stop its destructive behavior.

The Golem Effect creates self-fulfilling prophecies, just like the Pygmalion and Galatea Effects—only these are negative ones. In education, as an example, when a 5th grade teacher tells a 6th grade teacher how poorly a student did in her class, the 6th grade teacher holds much lower expectations about how well that student will do in his class. In management this can be seen in the negative or low expectations held by one's supervisor that are believed to influence an employee to demonstrate lower performance that he is capable of. These findings have held true across multiple studies.[10]

At its worst, the Golem Effect results in less attention and less feedback given to the targeted employees. Moreover, by conveying these expectations across the organization to other managers and employees, the self-fulfilling prophecy (positive or negative) is perpetuated. Either way, it can serve either as motivation to rise to the level of others' expectations, or it can be a de-motivating factor that leads to lower engagement and performance at work.

The bottom line is that managers have the ability to influence how their direct reports approach their tasks and engage with their jobs and relationships. Telling employees that they believe in them or delegating important tasks to them conveys a positive message about their value and performance. Conveying with raised eyebrows their disappointment in someone's performance or dismissing the person's ideas in a meeting conveys a manager's negative impression of that employee. It is important to recognize that self-fulfilling prophecies are powerful influences that partially determine how much effort employees will choose to expend on their tasks, as well as in cultivating and maintaining work relationships.

In the next section you'll learn about two types of motivation—intrinsic motivation and extrinsic motivation—and discover the power each has in determining how much effort employees exert toward achieving their goals.

The Superior Power of Intrinsic Motivation

The two different types of motivation are based on the different reasons or goals that propel people to behave. As Ryan and Deci describe them, "the most basic distinction is between *intrinsic* motivation, which refers to doing something because it is inherently interesting or enjoyable, and *extrinsic* motivation, which refers to doing something because it leads to a separable outcome. Over three decades of research has shown that the quality of experience and performance can be very different when one is behaving for intrinsic versus extrinsic reasons."[11]

In the 20th century most organizations were much more attuned to motivating employees using extrinsic rewards, such as pay, promotions, benefits, job security, pensions, and so on. These address some basic needs that

---

[10] See for example, Judice, T. N. and Neuberg, S.L. (1998). When interviewers desire to confirm negative expectations: Self-fulfilling prophecies and inflated applicant self-perceptions. *Basic & Applied Social Psychology,* 20, 3,175–190.

[11] See review by Ryan, R.M. and Deci, E.L. (2000). Intrinsic and extrinsic motivations: Classic definitions and new directions. *Contemporary Educational Psychology* 25, 54–67. doi:10.1006/ceps.1999.1020.

all employees have, including being able to support one's family and to gain some overall financial security. While these are still important to a degree, the sustainability of these externally-derived rewards is limited with regard to their motivational potential. *In essence, when the reward changes or no longer addresses a critical need, its ability to motivate decreases.*

Additionally, the power of extrinsic rewards is dependent on the type of work one is rewarding. For those types of jobs that require routine, rule-based tasks for which there is one solution or goal, extrinsic motivators (like money) work fairly well, because they make very clear for employees what they will get when they achieve the required result. This approach has worked particularly well in manufacturing organizations. For example, *piece work* is a system that pays employees for the number of things they make or the number of tasks they complete. Employees are very clear how much per piece or per task they will earn. Thus, they become very focused on producing the number required to get the reward, but they may not be as concerned with the quality of what is produced, since they are not being rewarded for quality.

But for more professional, creative endeavors in which you want employees to broaden their search for multiple alternative solutions or to produce an unspecified outcome, extrinsic motivators tend to work against that goal. Imagine if you told a research scientist that you would pay her only when she conducted six experiments? She would be motivated merely to conduct the six experiments, not to find a viable cure for a disease.

Professional employees are driven to expend effort because work is interesting, challenging, and absorbing, all of which are essential for high levels of creativity. Therefore, intrinsic motivators are usually more powerful than extrinsic motivators in keeping employees engaged with their work.

Daniel Pink, in his best-selling book, *Drive*, challenges organizations to ignore intrinsic motivation at their peril.[12] He maintains that there are three powerful intrinsic motivators that are essential for 21st century employees: Autonomy, Mastery, and Purpose.

Autonomy, according to Pink, means acting with choice, which he argues is not the same as working independently. Work that includes the ability to be autonomous does not preclude that we can also enjoy working interdependently with others. To be intrinsically motivating, autonomy must be experienced across multiple aspects of a job: in what an employee does, how she does it, when she does it, and with whom she does it. As a result, the ability for employees to be self-directed creates more engagement and motivation.

---

[12] Pink, D. H. (2009). *Drive: The surprising truth about what motivates us.* New York, NY: Riverhead Books.

Mastery, Pink claims, is "the capacity to see your abilities not as finite, but as infinitely improvable."[13] Carol Dweck would agree. In her book, *Mindset,*[14] Dweck demonstrated that those who believe intelligence is genetically fixed are less likely to push themselves and, consequently, restrict their growth potential. Conversely, those who believe intelligence can be developed take risks, push themselves to do better, and out-perform those with a more fixed mindset. Ironically, the motivational potential that mastery provides is in its elusiveness; as Pink notes, "the joy is in the pursuit more than the realization. In the end, mastery attracts precisely because mastery eludes." Although mastery is important for all professionals, the millennial generation finds mastery particularly motivating, and the more developmental opportunities available, the more that younger employees will find their jobs engaging.

Purpose is the desire to do things in service of something larger than ourselves. Because we spend so much time working, it is important for us to believe that what we do matters. And for the millennial generation, this requirement is as important as any other for engagement in their work. For example, in 2016 Gallup released the results of a survey that focused on millennials.[15] Gallup discovered roughly half of the generation values things other than salary when searching for a new job, and growth and development opportunities head the list.

As a manager, your purpose is to serve the greater good by bringing people and resources together to create value that no single individual can create alone. From a motivational and an engagement perspective, when you create opportunities for employees to focus on something greater than themselves, they will. This is beginning to be a major focus in organizations, particularly those that have increased their involvement as volunteers in civic and non-profit organizations. For example, many business organizations pay their employees to take time off to volunteer at various non-profits. The non-profit benefits, and the business organizations are also seeing benefits as a result, such as increased trust among employees, greater employee self-awareness, higher employee engagement, and lower employee turnover.[16] Managers who

---

[13] Pink, p. 83.

[14] Dweck, C.S. (2008). *Mindset: The new psychology of success.* New York, NY: Ballantine Books.

[15] The Gallup survey results can be downloaded for free at https://news.gallup.com/reports/189830/e.aspx?utm_source=gbj&utm_medium=copy&utm_campaign=20160601-gbj

[16] Gay, W. (2016). 4 reasons why a corporate volunteer program is a smart investment. *Forbes,* November 3. Retrieved from https://www.forbes.com/sites/wesgay/2016/11/03/4-reasons-why-a-corporate-volunteer-program-is-a-smart-investment/, June 28, 2018.

can provide more opportunities for intrinsic motivation and who create a culture that values more creative, engaged employees will experience many of these same benefits.

When Organizational Reward Systems Mess It All Up

At this point you certainly can see that managers play a crucial role in creating an environment where employees can be engaged and motivated to do their best work. However, there are times when the best managers in the world, the most talented employees available, and all the resources necessary to accomplish the organization's goals still cannot seem to sustain employees' motivation and engagement.

Why is this?

The answer lies in a very simple principle of motivation—basically, that people do what they are rewarded for doing—which is described in the classic 1975 article by Steven Kerr *On the Folly of Rewarding A While Hoping for B*.[17] In his article Kerr describes this as "… reward systems that are fouled up in that behaviors which are rewarded are those which the rewarder is trying to *discourage*, while the behavior he desires is not being rewarded at all." This can be found in organizations at all levels.

For example, many of you might have worked with a budget. Budgets represent an estimate of income (money that comes in) and expenses (money that goes out). By their very nature budgets are designed to allocate money to those things that the organization needs and values. In business, most departments are allocated a certain amount of money for specific things: salaries, travel, office supplies, copying, etc. The budget represents what the organization is allowing you to spend. However, at the end of the budget period (usually a year), if you have been a very efficient and effective manager, you may have money left over, which you would think the organization would appreciate and reward …. right?

However, in most companies the efficient and effective manager, who believes that the organization "hoped" he would save as much money as he could, finds that the organization scoops up the remaining balance of his budget, leaving him with $0 at the end of the year. Then, he discovers that in the next year's budget the amount allocated is reduced by the amount he saved the previous year!

Now what do you think this manager does in the next budget cycle?

That's right, he spends every last penny he is allocated. Why? Because although the organization "hopes" he will be as effective and efficient with his

---

[17] Kerr, S. (1975). On the folly of rewarding A, while hoping for B. *The Academy of Management Journal*, 18, 769–783.

next budget, he is "rewarded" for spending it all. That is the power of "rewarding A while hoping for B."

When organizations set up reward systems that reward the very thing they don't want, it wreaks havoc with the other motivational tools that managers have, including extrinsic and intrinsic rewards. As Kerr concludes, "Managers who complain that their workers are not motivated might do well to consider the possibility that they have installed reward systems which are paying off for behaviors other than those they are seeking."

Concluding Thoughts

Every manager can benefit from understanding why employees become disengaged and de-motivated so that they don't jump to solutions before they understand the causes of the problem. Employees are complicated. They are not all motivated by the same things, but almost all of them are de-motivated by similar aspects of their tasks and workplaces. And that is where good managers can help:

- By being honest and authentic about how employees' skills fit the job requirements,

- By making sure employees know they are valued and appreciated,

- By providing those who seek them, opportunities for growth and development,

- By insuring that the organization itself isn't rewarding the very things it claims it doesn't want, and

- By always being trustworthy and ethical in your treatment of your employees.

Whether your employees are motivated or de-motivated, you will need to provide feedback about their skills, behaviors, and required outcomes. This role—"Manager as Evaluator"—is an important one for both you and your direct reports. And it doesn't consist of just doing a yearly performance appraisal. It is much more than that, as you will see in Chapter 9.

Additional Reading, Resources, and Activities

In order to get the most out of what you've already read, the following are some additional helpful resources and activities.

- View videos on YouTube or TedX, or watch popular movies that illustrates the power of intrinsic and extrinsic rewards. Then discuss ways to create a more motivational environment in an organization, particularly for multigenerational employees.

- Dead Poet's Society, Remember the Titans, Dangerous Minds

- The Death Crawl (https://www.youtube.com/watch?v=-sUKoKQlEC4)

- Daniel Pink on The Science of Motivation (https://www.youtube.com/watch?v=esvaP9LehB4)

- The Sid Story (http://www.crmlearning.com/the-sid-story) – this must be purchased from CRM Learning, but it is very good at demonstrating self-fulfilling prophecy.

- Read the original article "On the Folly of Rewarding A While Hoping for B." How do grades represent what educational institutions "hope" students gain vs. what students are actually "rewarded" for? What would you suggest might work better?

- Take a piece of paper and draw a line down the middle. On the left side list those things that motivate you; on the right side list those things that de-motivate you. Are there any patterns to the lists? How does your chosen profession reflect what you've listed on each? What questions would you ask an interviewer to make sure your motivational preferences will be available in a new job?

Manager as Evaluator

Every defeat, every heartbreak, every loss, contains its own seed, its own lesson on how to improve your performance the next time.

—*Malcolm X, human rights advocate (1925–1965)*

It is likely that your performance has been evaluated at some time in your life, whether it was by a parent, a teacher, a coach, or a supervisor. You may have received an evaluation by your parent for how well you've cleaned your room, or from your ballet teacher on how precisely you are able to pirouette. Coaches evaluate our swings, kicks, grips, and stances. We have all received comments from teachers on how well or poorly we've written an essay, and the ultimate evaluation in school we've all experienced are the grades that are intended to indicate how well we have achieved the objectives for the class.

Think for a moment about what your experiences have been in the evaluations you've experienced:

- Were they pleasant or harsh?
- Were they helpful or hurtful?
- Did your performance change (for better or worse) as a result of the evaluations?

One of the most important roles that managers have is to provide feedback about their direct reports' performance in their jobs and then to make an evaluation of how well or poorly they have performed. The idea underlying all of this is to help their subordinates improve their performance, but it is also intended to help them see where their skills and competencies need improvement, as well as to identify additional talents and gifts that they might develop further.

Unfortunately, many managers both dread and fear conducting performance evaluations, and there are several reasons for this.

Why Managers Dread Performance Evaluations

The first (and, in my opinion, the most likely) reason is that managers have never really been trained how to do them. It would be like asking someone to change the oil in a car without first showing them where the oil filter is, how to drain the oil, and what type of replacement oil and filter to use. While they may stumble into figuring it out, there could be irreparable damage to the car's engine in the process. So, too, can performance evaluations cause damage to employees' motivation and self-esteem when they are done incorrectly.

Another reason that managers don't like evaluating someone's performance is that they aren't always that familiar with the job or the person they are evaluating. They might have basic knowledge of the purpose for the job, but many managers often have never actually done the job themselves. In other words, job incumbents often know the job better than those who are evaluating their performance in it, and this makes for an uncomfortable situation on the part of both the evaluator and the person being evaluated.

Moreover, for jobs in which the manager rarely has the opportunity to observe performance, the manager may not have full information about how well the employees perform the job or if they actually demonstrate the skills and behaviors required. This is particularly true for remote employees, those who telecommute, and those whose jobs require them to be on the road or away from the office most of the time.

Some managers also fear conducting job evaluations because they see them as confrontational. Sitting down with a direct report and providing any negative feedback or judgment about performance can be very unnerving for managers who try to avoid potential conflict situations. And for managers who are not very skilled at interpersonal communication, even talking with subordinates about anything can be stressful.

Even if managers enjoy the interaction with their employees, a further reason they dread actually doing evaluations is that they usually don't enjoy the bureaucratic process that it entails. In essence, it is often seen as extra work that gets in the way of their "real" work. And when managers have a lot of direct reports, they often spend hours filling in forms, writing comments, reviewing records, conducting discussions, and then submitting all the accompanying paperwork.

All of these reasons and more conspire against the healthy process of providing constructive performance feedback and evaluation to employees. But before we advocate getting rid of the process because of all these poor perceptions and fears, let's take a look at how a different approach can make the process more pleasant, more productive, and more beneficial for both managers and employees alike. This entails a holistic approach to managing every aspect of an employee's performance, one that has come to be known as *performance management*.

What Is Performance Management?

The term *performance management* means more than just filling out a performance review once a year. Rather, it is designed to promote ongoing communication between a manager and employee regarding the planning and achieving of workplace goals; the clear understanding of the job's requirements; the knowledge, skills, abilities, and competencies[1] that are necessary for an employee's successful job performance; and the identification of areas for improvement and development.

There are four separate focus areas in performance management:

- Performance planning—identification of behaviors and results that define performance,
- Performance measurement—creation of measures that are valid and reliable indicators of those behaviors and results,
- Performance evaluation—engagement in the process of giving feedback and providing evaluation about performance of the behaviors and results, and
- Performance development—coaching employees on developing more effective behaviors and skills so that their performance results will continue to improve.

All four of these steps require an understanding the organization's mission, vision, and strategy, transparency, and clarity of what "effective performance" means, and system-wide cooperation and commitment to performance and skill improvement. Let's explore the first three of these in more detail. The next chapter, "Manager as Coach," will deal exclusively with the fourth step.

Planning Performance

One of the most important parts of performance management is to make sure that employees know what is expected of them. That is, managers must plan for the desired outcomes (results) and the means of achieving them (behaviors). If we look at the process of performance planning, we find the following

---

[1] We use the terms "knowledge, skills, abilities" to describe what a job incumbent is capable of doing. The term "competencies" is used to describe actual behaviors that demonstrate a job incumbent's level of mastery at performing job requirements.

sequence makes a lot of sense from an organization's strategic point of view (Figure 1):

The process begins with the senior leadership setting the strategic goals for the overall organization during a specific time period; that is, "Which" goals are to be achieved? Next, the strategies for achieving the goals are developed; that is, "How" we will achieve the goals? This is referred to as strategic planning, and organizations typically engage in this process annually, and, in many organizations, every 3–5 years senior leaders set longer-term goals and strategies.

Once strategic planning is complete for the specific time horizon, the senior leadership gives each department or unit the overall goals and strategies. At this point, each unit develops its own goals and strategies that, once achieved, will allow the organization to meet the overall goals. As strategic management gurus are often fond of saying, "Goals are set from the top down, but they are achieved from the bottom up."

The departments and units then look at what they are trying to achieve and how they plan on achieving it, and the managers ask a very important question: "Do we have the right jobs and positions (job incumbents) in place that will allow us to carry out our strategies?" The answer is found by looking at the job descriptions that presumably identify the tasks required, as well as the knowledge, skills, and competencies that are necessary to conduct those tasks. If the answer is "no," then recruitment and selection activities need to occur. But if the answer is "yes," then managers must work with the job

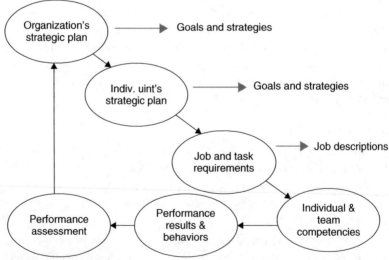

Figure 1 Linking Performance Planning and Strategy

Source: Dale J. Dwyer

incumbents to identify the parts that each will commit to so that the department (and ultimately, the overall organization) will be able to achieve its goals. This commitment results in establishing key accountability areas for each job, performance standards for each key accountability area, individual performance goals, and, perhaps, skill and competency improvement goals.

For example, as a manager of a marketing department, you may take the organization's overall goal of "increase market share of Product A by 10% next year," and construct your department's goal as "increase purchases by females who are 25–35 years old by 10% next year." You then construct your strategy, for example, how to increase the reach of advertisements that will be targeted to that demographic.

However, when you look at the staff in your advertising department, you may find that you don't have any advertising expertise or experience in that demographic currently on staff. You then proceed to specify the particular knowledge and skills required for a new staff member, as well as to identify the behavioral competencies and performance standards that would signify what a successful and competent job performance would look like for someone in that job. Once a person is hired and informed about the competencies and performance standards for the job, you construct measures of the specific behaviors and results against which the new marketing staff member will be assessed.

As you can see from the diagram, all of this assessment is then fed back up to senior leaders who, after determining whether the overall organizational goals were met, proceed to start the whole process all over again. Performance planning, therefore, is an iterative process that uses individual and unit performance as feedback for how well or how poorly the strategies worked to achieve the desired results for the organization.

Likewise, individual performance planning adopts the same process: identify desired individual results, determine individual behaviors and competencies that are needed, evaluate achievement of the individual results, and either refine the goals or provide training and development to help employees' ability and mastery so that they will be able to achieve them the next time around.

Measuring Performance

The second part of performance management involves having measures so that employees are clear about what level of performance they are being held accountable for, and managers are able to gauge performance against a standard. To construct performance measures that are *valid*, meaning that they measure what they are intended to measure and that are *reliable*, meaning that they are consistent over time and with multiple job incumbents, is no easy task. In fact, many organizations do not have the expertise in house to do this, and so they rely on measures that are purchased from consulting firms or publishers. While this approach may work, often these measures are so generic as to be useless. It is a complex, but not impossible, task to construct your own.

How to construct performance measures. Once you have a job description that lists detailed and specific job and task requirements, as well as specific knowledge and skill requirements for the job incumbent, it is just a matter of determining the level of mastery that might be demonstrated by a job incumbent. These levels are typically designated so that they clearly differentiate among the levels (e.g., "meets standards [M]," "exceeds standards [E]," and "falls below standards [B]") of the performance standards you expect. This is necessary so that evaluators know what they are actually looking for in judging a person's performance, and the mastery levels of that performance will be clearly spelled out for the job incumbent.

Here is an example for one key accountability area called "Facilities Operation":

Key Accountability Area: Facilities Operation		Weight: 10%	
Key Essential Functions	**Performance Mastery Levels**	**Employee Rating**	**Manager Rating**
Conduct routine maintenance inspections of the building. Work with housekeeping and maintenance crews to ensure the completion of repairs. Maintain accurate individual and group billing information and deposit records for damages. Work with Environmental Affairs in fire protection procedures.	**Below expectations:** Collaboration and building inspections usually get delayed or resisted by employee. Record keeping tends to be chaotic. **Meets expectations:** Accurately meets deadlines for inspections. Effectively collaborate and work with other crews. Records are accurate and organized. **Exceeds expectations:** Conducts inspections routinely and when problems are suspected. Continually building good relationships with other crews. Records and procedures are always up-to-date.	B M E ■ ■ ■ 1 3 5 Rating (1,3, or 5) × 10%= _____	B M E ■ ■ ■ 1 3 5 Rating (1,3, or 5) × 10%= _____
Comments: _____ _____ _____ _____			

Source: Dale J. Dwyer

Notice how the "Key Essential Functions" are really the tasks that matter the most in the job. These come directly from the job description. Also note that the "Mastery Performance Levels" capture the significant aspects of performance in that function that indicate whether a job incumbent had met, exceeded, or fallen short of expectations.

You might also note that this particular score is weighted by 10%. Given that there are five to seven essential functions for most jobs (some have more, of course), weighting them provides a job incumbent with a sense of how important each one is in relation to the others identified for the overall job. It also provides a more valid and fair performance evaluation, since it makes clear that not every function is as important as every other one.

The decision to measure behaviors or results. It is worth mentioning here that every job has both behaviors and results that can be measured and evaluated. Some jobs are more dependent on "how" someone performs the job, and some jobs are more dependent on the "what" that results from those behaviors. If we can observe how the job incumbent does the job, behaviors may be more important to evaluate. But if we don't have the opportunity of observing how they do the job, perhaps it is better to rely on results to judge employees' performance.

Let's use a hospital nurse as an example of the former. One of the key essential functions of a nurse might be "setting up IVs for patients." We can easily observe as the nurse implants the port into the patient's arm, makes sure the IV bag has the correct contents, places the bag correctly on the pole holder, and starts the IV drip at the right speed. In other words, we can observe "how" the nurse has mastered this key function, and we can evaluate the nurse's performance on those behaviors. However, even if the nurse does all of these things absolutely 100% correctly, it is still possible the patient could get sicker or even die. In other words, the nurse's behaviors do not completely determine the outcome, and we surely don't want to hold the nurse accountable for either of those outcomes!

On the other hand, it would be highly unusual to be able to observe all the behaviors of sales reps (e.g., planning sales calls, delivering a sales pitch, writing a proposal, following up, etc.), since no one is with them most of the time they are doing them. In this case, it would be more appropriate to rely on the results of these behaviors, that is "Number of completed sales calls" or "Total sales $." Because we can't observe a sales person actually doing the job, the only performance metrics we have are outcomes. However, the presumption is that the sales rep's behaviors are directly related to the outcomes—improvement in any of the behaviors will lead to a greater number and dollar amount of sales.

Of course, once you have these done for all the jobs for which you will be conducting a performance evaluation, it is just a matter of deciding how you will conduct the actual evaluation and feedback meeting itself. This is Step 3 in our process.

Evaluating Performance

There are two basic types of performance evaluation: the *summative* evaluation and the *formative* evaluation. In a summative evaluation, the evaluator looks at the total of the performance across all key functional areas and then assigns one overall score. You are likely very used to getting summative evaluations in school. At the end of a course, the instructor totals up the scores for all your assignments, homework, exams, projects, and papers, and then gives you one grade for the term. In essence, the instructor provides one summary score of your overall performance in the course.

In business, we often see summative evaluations. After providing training, for example, we may measure several things:

- Whether the trainees actually learned the material,
- How the trainees actually use the information they learned, and
- Whether the trainees' quality or quantity of work has changed as a result of the training.

All of these are overall evaluations of an individual's performance as a result of training. In addition, summative evaluations are often done for the training program itself to see whether the program needs tweaked or improved in its design or delivery.

In evaluating job performance, summative evaluations can be given quarterly, semiannually, or annually to assess whether employees have met their goals, have improved on certain behaviors, or are ready for promotion to higher-level jobs. The bottom line is that most *managers use summative evaluations to make employment decisions* about employees, such as raises, bonuses, and promotions or, in some cases, demotions, discipline, and termination. Here is an example of a summary performance evaluation. Note that it results in one overall score being given (1, 2, 3, 4, or 5) (Figure 2):

☐ Unacceptable 1	☐ Needs improvement 2	☐ Meets expectations 3	☐ Exceeds expectations 4	☐ Outstanding 5
Work performance is inadequate and consistently falls below the standards of performance required for the position. Performance at this level requires an improvement plan.	Work performance occasionally does not meet the standards of performance required. Serious effort is needed to improve performance.	Work performance consistently meets the standards of performance for the position.	Work performance is often above the standards of performance for the position.	Work performance consistently exceeds the standards required for the position.

Figure 2 Example of Summary Performance Evaluation

Source: Dale J. Dwyer

In contrast, formative evaluations provide information so that an employee's performance behaviors can be adjusted or improved while they can still have an impact on the goals or results to be achieved. For example, some instructors give midterm course evaluations, asking the students to indicate if there is anything the instructor should "stop" doing, "start" doing, or "change" before the course ends. This allows the instructor to correct a technique that isn't working well, to refrain from doing something annoying, or to add more instruction or explanation than is currently provided.

In classes, you have probably taken short quizzes to see whether you have grasped the main points of a topic. Perhaps you have been asked to do a one-minute writing assignment to assess whether you understand the basics of supply and demand in economics, or maybe you have participated in a clicker poll during a class to see if the whole class understands an accounting standard. These are all formative assessments that allow the instructor to get quick feedback on what they need to be explained more thoroughly or what a student needs to study more intently.

In business, we often use formative evaluations to identify skills or competencies that employees need to develop, to identify high-potential candidates for leadership training, or to generally discuss one's potential for career advancement. As you will see in the next chapter, *managers use formative performance evaluations to provide the foundation for employee improvement, development, and career success.*

Before we leave this topic, however, it is important to make sure that in your "manager as evaluator" role you are able to communicate the feedback so that your employees can hear and understand what you are telling them. To do this, you will need to understand a bit more about feedback and tips for conducting the actual evaluation meeting.

Giving and Receiving Feedback

For over 25 years, management researchers have extolled the benefits for employees who actively seek feedback from their managers, colleagues, and the environment they work in.[2] In fact, research into feedback-seeking has been encouraged as a means to not only improve performance but also to boost feelings of self-efficacy and mastery.

Feedback-seeking behavior is particularly useful for newer employees who already have high self-efficacy and who have a high learning goal

---

[2] Ashford, S. J., & Cummings, L. L. (1983). Feedback as an individual resource: Personal strategies of creating information. *Organizational Behavior and Human Performance, 32,* 370–398.

orientation. Moreover, if such employees perceive the source of the feedback (e.g., manager and colleagues) as credible and trustworthy, they are more likely to seek information about how well they are perceived to be doing in their jobs.[3]

While there are many employees who actively seek feedback about their performance, there are also many who fear receiving feedback and many managers who dread providing it. However, learning how to give and receive feedback is crucial. Everyone wins when employees <u>and</u> managers seek feedback, because their work becomes more aligned with the organization's goals, and they are able to create a more open and honest environment to improve performance. One aspect to improving feedback is to prepare in advance for the evaluation and feedback meeting.

Preparing for the Performance Feedback and Evaluation Meeting

One of the frequent mistakes managers often make is that they are not prepared for the meeting itself. Preparation is key to making sure that you know all the aspects you want to discuss and that your employees are also prepared to discuss their performance with you.

There are several steps managers should take prior to having a meeting to evaluate a direct report.

1. **Refresh your memory on the events, issues, and so on that you plan to discuss**. If you think you can give specific feedback on a wide range of behaviors or results without this preparation, you are wrong. This is crucial to ensuring that employees get information about their performance across the full spectrum. If you only can remember the most recent great (or poor) thing they have done, you are not being fair.

2. **Give the employees ample notice of the meeting**. Most employees are busy, as are their managers. By making sure they have plenty of time to prepare what they want to talk about and not be rushed, you will have a much more fruitful discussion.

3. **Allow employees to comment about their own performance on the evaluation**. It is a good practice to get employees' own ideas about where their strengths and challenges lie. You may be surprised at their

---

[3] Anseel, F., Beatty, A. S., Shen, W., Lievens, F., & Sackett, P. R. (2015). How are we doing after 30 years? A meta-analytic review of the antecedents and outcomes of feedback-seeking behavior. *Journal of Management, 41*(1), 318–348. doi:10.1177/0149206313484521

responses, and they may not agree with your own. This also gives you the ability to talk through the differences in your perceptions.

4. **Arrange a private place to meet, free from distractions**. This is crucial. No one wants to be considered an inconvenience! By making sure your one-on-one with your employees is not interrupted by email, texts, phone calls, or knocks on your door, you can be fully present to them. They will feel as if they are truly being heard, and you will be able to concentrate on ensuring you have the time and temperament to have the crucial conversations that provide instructive feedback for performance improvement.

5. **Allow enough time for the evaluation, discussion, and a few minutes for you to document the meeting.** In addition to having a quiet, uninterrupted space, managers need to allot enough time, not only for the feedback session itself, but also to record what happened and what was agreed to in the discussion. This is important for two reasons. First, rushing a performance discussion makes it difficult to get all the concerns and details fully discussed. Second, rushing a feedback session conveys a sense that it is only a formality and not an important part of your job. Neither one of these conditions sends a positive message to your employees that they are valued.

In addition to these preparatory steps, there are several things one must do during a performance discussion:

1. DO recognize what the employee has done well.
2. DO tactfully point out what the employee could do better.
3. DO be specific and give examples.
4. DO be encouraging.
5. DO listen to employee's concerns and observations.
6. DO set expectations for future behavior and results.

Likewise, there are several things you should avoid doing during a performance evaluation:

1. DON'T compare the employee to others.
2. DON'T dwell on past mistakes; rather, concentrate on what can happen in the future.
3. DON'T belittle the person. Choose vocabulary wisely.
4. DON'T ask intimidating questions; for example, "Why didn't you . . .?"
5. DON'T make promises you may not be able to keep, for example, raise, bonus, promotion.

Concluding Thoughts

Your employees need to understand how and why they have done well. It isn't enough to imply, "as long as you don't hear differently, keep doing what you're doing." Whether they inherently seek feedback or not, providing honest and instructive feedback motivates them to improve their performance and, at the very least, gives both the manager and the employees an opportunity to understand each other better.

Now, let's turn to the last managerial role, "Manager as Coach." You will be able to see how performance evaluation and feedback are used to help employees grow and develop their gifts and talents even further. And that is the ultimate gift you, as a manager, can give your staff.

Additional Reading, Resources, and Activities

In order to get the most out of what you've already read, the following are some additional helpful resources and activities.

- If your instructor is open to it, practice giving feedback on a specific aspect of your class (e.g., book used, style of teaching, class rules, exercises used, etc.) In this session, make sure you follow the "Do's and Don'ts" presented in the chapter.

- Read the article, Jackman, J. M., & Strober, M. H. (2003, April). Fear of feedback. *Harvard Business Review*,. After reading the article, discuss why it might be that so many people, including managers and employees, fear giving and receiving feedback.

Manager as Coach

10

It's not what the coach knows; it is what his players have learned.

—Anonymous

For those of us who have played a sport, learned to sing, dance, or play an instrument, or have worked to improve our academic skills, we probably have had a coach. Our experience with a coach might consist of a patient and motivating person who took great pride in our accomplishments. On the other hand, we may have experienced a coach who yelled, demeaned us in front of our peers, and was more focused on his or her own personal gain than on our development and growth. Whatever our experiences have been with coaching, as a manager one of the most important roles you will undertake will be to help your employees become better at what they do and, sometimes, to help them realize that what they are currently doing is not what they really want to do or should be doing.

That's right. Sometimes a good coach must point out when someone is not cut out for a particular sport, art form, academic pursuit, or job. As part of coaching, managers engage in encouraging their employees toward lifetime learning and development. In fact, the most direct connection managers have with their employees is often through employee development planning and coaching.

The benefits of coaching can be seen in increased business performance and employee engagement, according to a 2015 survey from the International Coach Federation (ICF) and the Human Capital Institute (HCI).[1] The survey found that 51 percent of respondents from organizations with strong coaching cultures reported revenue above that of their industry peer group, and 62 percent of employees in those organizations rated themselves as highly engaged.

---

[1] Human Capital Institute, in partnership with International Coach Federation. (2016). *Building a coaching culture with managers and leaders*. Retrieved from http://www.hci.org/files/field_content_file/2016%20ICF.pdf

The purpose of coaching is to foster employee growth and development. One of the misnomers about employee development is that it is basically just training. In fact, many times we hear the phrase "training and development," and we might think they are one and the same. But they are different in several ways.

What is Training?

The first difference between training and employee development is that training is *focused on learning* a *specific skill or knowledge*. For example, we might be trained in how to use a spreadsheet, how to give a PowerPoint presentation, or how to run a specific machine. As managers, we often train new employees on how to do something that is specific to our organizations: how to use the company's human resource portal, how to complete monthly sales reports, or how to process a product returned by a customer to inventory.

The second difference is that training is focused on the here and now. In essence, training is *meant for the short-term acquisition of skills and knowledge*. As employees gain the specific skill or some particular knowledge, they are able to apply it immediately to their required tasks. For example, training an employee how to complete her monthly sales report implies that she will do it correctly and submit it when it is due next month.

The third difference is that training is *organization-driven*, that is to say that the organization requires its employees to be able to do and know the specific skills and knowledge. Therefore, the organization is responsible for organizing, paying for, and delivering (or hiring someone to deliver) the training. Unfortunately, sometimes training is not well done, although the organization still requires employees to attend. If employees wish to continue on in the job, they are basically required to attend the training—whether or not they actually learn anything!

Organizations decide on what training an employee needs to be successful in a specific job and requests or compels the employee to acquire job-specific skills and knowledge. This is very different from developing an employee's competencies, gifts, and talents for a career.

What is Employee Development?

Employee development is practically the opposite of training. Whereas training focuses on required job-specific skills and knowledge, employee development is *geared to the individual employee's interests and talents*. Its purpose is to build a successful professional over his or her career in a variety of jobs and levels in organizations of all types.

As a result, unlike training that insures a short-term result in skill or knowledge acquisition, employee development *focuses on the long-term career path of the individual.* Development goals are much broader and generally focus on behavioral competencies that are wider-ranging. For example, employee development might deal with competencies such as improving one's emotional intelligence, developing leadership skills, or learning the best ways to change a culture.

Finally, one of the biggest differences between training and employee development is that the latter is *driven by the individual employee, not the organization.* Development programs are highly personalized plans that require a long-term commitment to self-learning and practice by the employee. As we will discuss next, these plans can involve formal and informal learning, as well as professional and personal experiential situations.

Planning for Employee Development

In many organizations that offer employee development opportunities, the process often begins early in the tenure of the employee. As we have already learned, performance feedback and evaluation provide the manager and the employee with the ongoing ability to assess skills and knowledge. But it also permits them to begin planning for longer and more advanced career goals.

The planning usually begins with some sort of an inventory of the employee's skills, talents, and interests. Here are some starter questions that may help the employee with a personal assessment:

1. What am I good at?
2. What am I interested in?
3. What do I need to work on?
4. What would help me at this point?
5. What might hinder my progress?

The next major question is "Where do I want to be?" or "What is my ultimate goal?" Issues to address in this part of the planning might include how much time, effort, money, and motivation an employee is willing to invest in the process. Obviously, if the organization is encouraging the employee to pursue developmental goals, the amount of support the employee's organization and manager are willing to provide is also an important consideration. It is often the case that family support is also required, particularly if the employee's long-term career goals involve money, travel, education, relocation, and time commitments that will affect family members.

The final planning part of an employee's development is to set some short-term and long-term goals. For example, a short-term goal may involve completing a particular course or certification, while a long-term goal might be to get promoted to a management role, take on an important long-term project, or accept a global assignment.

Once these steps have all been completed initially, it is time to think about the actual developmental activities that will improve the competencies required to achieve the short-term and long-term goals. To that end, here is a list of some potential example activities:

Formal Education	Work Experiences
• Individual classes • Degree programs • Continuing education workshops and seminars • Action research	• Job rotations • Challenging projects • Ad hoc problem-solving teams • Coaching or mentoring another person
Informal Education	Non-work Experiences
• Maintaining a reflective learning journal • Reading professional books and journals • Attending meetings of professional group or society • Creating a study group around a topic	• Volunteering in the community • Serving in civic or religious organizations • Mentoring youth • Coaching a sport or an academic area

You will notice that they fall into four separate categories: Educational activities (both formal and informal) and Experiential activities (both work and non-work). These are just examples, of course. There are many other activities that may be appropriate and helpful for the employee, and managers can help employees think through the possibilities that might be engaging and helpful for them. Creativity and engagement are valued in employee development!

Coaching Style

As noted at the beginning of this chapter, we all have our ideas for what it means to coach or be coached. However, a manager who takes on the role of coach must keep in mind that every employee will differ in how he or she likes to be coached and how well each employee receives coaching. To have only one approach to coaching may leave some of your employees unresponsive.

To illustrate, consider how people learn. For some, they need only to hear or read about what you expect from them to be able to apply what you are suggesting. For others, they must see someone actually doing it and then model that person's behavior. For others, they must actually engage in doing it themselves before they understand fully how to do it. As an example, think about how you like to get directions when you are lost:

- Do you understand where you are and where you are going just by looking at a map?
- Can you only know where to go if someone draws you a picture or writes down every street turn and landmark between where you are and where you want to be?
- Are you able to listen to directions verbally and find your way?

Depending on how you learn, coaching works like this, too. Sometimes the coach can tell an employee what she might need to do differently, but other employees will need to see it done, have it put in writing, or just try experimenting themselves. The point here is that each employee will accept coaching from you differently, so you need to have a few tools in your toolbox to draw upon. Let's look at just three different approaches that could be used, depending upon the types of issues or employees you are dealing with.

Autocratic Coaching Style. This style requires the manager-coach to explain exactly what the employee needs to be doing differently and exactly how to do it. This approach works well for employees who need a lot of structure and accountability. It also works well when the behaviors required are very scripted or the outcome is too important to leave to chance. For example, coaching an employee who needs to develop a better customer-focused orientation may require that you give them specific approaches to use, rather than letting them develop their own by trial and error. An autocratic coaching style can also be helpful when there are legal, safety, or security consequences, such as making sure that employees have specific competencies for dealing with a potential workplace violence issue.

Democratic Coaching Style. A more democratic style invites the employee to participate in the coaching process. In essence, the employee adopts a self-coaching attitude in which the overall objective(s) are stated by the manager-coach, but the means of reaching them are suggested and adopted by the employee. This approach gives employees a sense of control and autonomy, while it also develops their ability to be introspective and to gain better decision-making skills. Employees who seek career coaching respond well to this approach, as do those who are trying to solve a problem that has more than one alternative solution.

Mindfulness Coaching Style. On occasion, some employees benefit greatly from learning how to reduce workplace tension, develop better relationships with others at work, improve their reactions to stressful situations, and generally achieve a healthier balance between work and non-work life spheres. "Mindfulness" refers to becoming more aware of yourself and of the world around you. Employees who are under a great deal of career or job stress, as well as those with attention deficit disorders may benefit from a mindfulness approach to coaching, as it improves their focus and retention.

There are myriad approaches to coaching, but as a manager who engages in coaching all types of employees, finding one that works for each individual approach is key. You will need to experiment to find not only what works with your employees, but also those approaches you feel comfortable using. If you are interested in learning how to become a better management or life coach, check out the International Coach Federation to learn more about credentialing and certification (http://coachfederation.org).

Not Doing Much Formal Coaching Yet?

As a newer manager, you may find that you are not asked to do much formal coaching. However, you can always adopt a coaching attitude with every employee who reports to you. Here are some ideas to make sure that your employees get the most out of your one-on-one discussions:

- **Be completely present to the employee while you are with him or her**. If you can't truly do this, reschedule for another time. They deserve 100% of your attention while you are talking with them about their performance.
- **Encourage employees to build on their strengths, don't just focus on their challenges**. Sometimes as managers we have a tendency to focus on what an employee can't do, rather than what they can do. However, we also forget that employees have strengths as well as challenges, and these can be used to help them work around some of the things they struggle with. For example, an employee who struggles with procrastination (a challenge) might be encouraged and coached in how to use his focus on details and plans (a strength) to help plan his projects so that he knows exactly when he must begin them to finish on time.
- **Be specific and comment on observable behaviors, not attitudes or personalities**. As manager-coaches we sometimes make the mistake of trying to change someone's attitude or personality trait. But that isn't really possible to do absent their desire to do so. Likewise, vague references to improvement or changes in behaviors aren't very effective, either. It isn't enough to say to an employee, "you need to improve on serving customers." Rather, it is much more helpful to say something like, "when you see a customer looking around, walk up to them to ask if you can help them find something." The more specific your comment and the more directly observable the behavior you wish to have the employee change,

the more likely the employee will be to adopt your suggestions or to come up with their own solutions to a problem behavior.

- **Check in to make sure you understand what he or she is saying**. Sometimes we think we know what the employee means, but we miss the mark. Even if you think you know, it is always better to make sure. For example, you can use these type of phrases: "When you say X, do you mean. . .?" or "Can you help me understand why you approached X the way you did?" When you ask for clarification, the employee feels as though you are really trying to understand his or her point of view.

- **Concentrate only on what can be changed, not on things that are out of the employee's control**. As mentioned a moment ago, attitudes and personalities are very difficult to change unless an employee really wants to change and undertakes the difficult work to do so. However, their behaviors are much more likely to be able to be modified. For example, asking a member of your wait staff to "be friendlier" is unrealistic. Suggesting that she "greet the customers, tell them your name, and suggest a favorite menu item" is perfectly realistic.

- **Give details and rationale for your comments**. Whether you are pointing out things the employee has done well or poorly, it is helpful to give an example that shows the employee what you focused on in your comments or evaluation: "The way you phrased that question was helpful to the client, because it gave him the opportunity to reflect on what he really needed from our firm." This provides the employee with a context, as well as details of why the behavior was appropriate or inappropriate.

- **Allow the other person to accept or reject your feedback**. As manager-coaches we cannot force employees to agree with everything we say. Coaching isn't about gaining compliance, it is about getting agreement. That is, coaching is about having the employees recognize that a problem exists and then agreeing with you that it is a problem and that they want to solve it. There may be valid reasons why your perceptions might be in error or your suggestions may not work for a particular employee or situation. Just as you are asking employees to be open to your suggestions and evaluation, you must be open to theirs as well.

Lessons From a Successful Coach

In order to give you a more complete picture of how a professional approaches coaching, I spoke with Ken Diaz, founder of Rock Fit in McLean, Virginia, about how he approaches fitness coaching. Although the topic might seem different than coaching an employee through a business problem or a performance issue, there are several commonalities that good manager-coaches have with successful professional fitness coaches as they engage with their clients. The following lessons that Ken shared may provide some insight into how you might plan with, and provide motivation for, your own employees. Here is what I learned from Ken about his approach to coaching:

1. A most important first step is to **have a conversation about goals**. This is more than just asking clients (or employees) about what they want to accomplish, although that is certainly important. But it is also assessing whether their expectations fit with what the coach can provide. As Ken recounted, a client who wants to improve her strength, stability, and endurance fits well with what he can provide as a coach; but a client who wants to become a body builder would not find his approach to fitness coaching sufficient. As manager-coaches we also want to make sure that our employees' expectations about their own development fit into the scope of what we can provide or support.

2. Another key aspect that Ken believes is important to successful coaching is to **assess motivation**. As he puts it, "we need to assess the WHY." Knowing why a client wants to work on her fitness or achieve a certain goal tells him a great deal about how diligent and persistent she will be, especially in the face of setbacks. As manager-coaches, knowing why an employee wants to pursue an advanced degree, an overseas assignment, or a more advanced position will let us know how deeply entrenched the value of development is for them. For fitness clients or our own employees, the more personal the reasons why development is meaningful to them, the more likely they will stick with it over the long haul. As their coach, we can help them remain accountable to their own plans and goals, but the motivation to continue is largely dependent on their own personal reasons for why those goals are meaningful to them.

3. **Challenge clients or employees to develop their own goals, plans, and strategies**. This gives them a sense of control and self-motivation. If a manager-coach is setting the goals and developing the plans, there is less engagement, as well as less "skin in the game" for the clients or employees. Interestingly, Ken also mentioned that he can tell how engaged a client is by listening to whether she describes her workouts as a "sacrifice" or an "investment." He notes that clients who see their workouts as "sacrifices" are generally less engaged, have more short-term goals (e.g., immediate weight loss rather than being fit for life), and may not stick with their fitness regimen if they don't see immediate results. Conversely, clients who consider their workouts as an "investment" in their overall quality of life are more engaged and persistent over the long haul. Likewise, manager-coaches should also be attuned to how employees view

and describe their own development plans and strategies. Do they see them as necessary steps to achieve a goal, or are they really interested in learning and developing competencies for more long-term growth and success? Assessing their long-term commitment is crucial for motivating continued successful employee development.

4. Development is a continual process in which our personal visions of ourselves evolve over time. As manager-coaches we need to **make room for both personal and professional growth** in our employees. When employees are able to see that their personal and career aspirations connect or, at least, are not at odds with one another, it is more likely that they will also be more satisfied. Asking the question, "how will this development benefit you overall as a person?" is a great way to get your employees thinking about the connection between both their work and non-work life spheres.

Concluding Thoughts

There is no more important role a manager plays than helping employees do their best work. In essence it is the main reason we are there: to help employees understand what their jobs entail and how they fit into the overall organization, to remove barriers that prevent them from doing those jobs, and to provide suggestions and resources to help them improve performance and reach their goals.

Sounds simple, doesn't it?

But as you have seen and, perhaps, experienced yourself, effective manager-coaches are not a dime a dozen. It is a skill that takes practice and training to develop, and good coaches work at it continually.

In the last chapter, as we wrap up our study of managerial roles, we'll review how these roles tie together. Importantly, the development of your own management competencies will be discussed so that you are able to continue to build on the fundamental skills you've learned here.

Additional Reading, Resources, and Activities

In order to get the most out of what you've already read, the following are some additional helpful resources and activities.

- Watch the movie, "Hoosiers" starring Gene Hackman, that is loosely based on a true basketball "Cinderella story" in 1954. In the movie, coach Norman Dale is fired from coaching a college basketball team because of his temper. Reluctantly, he is hired by a small Indiana high school and develops a whole new attitude about coaching. Pay particular attention to what he changed over the course of the movie about his approach to coaching.

- Think about times when you have been mentored or coached by someone who you admired and who really influenced development of the person you are today. Send them a thank-you note or letter and tell them the impact they have made on your life. Most people never hear enough about how they have influenced others!

- If you were interested in having a coach for your own professional growth and development, how might you answer the analysis questions posed earlier?

   1. What am I good at?

   2. What am I interested in?

   3. What do I need to work on?

   4. What would help me at this point?

   5. What might hinder my progress?

Developing Managerial Competency

11

What you do has far greater impact than what you say.

—*Stephen Covey*

Five Lessons Every Manager Needs to Learn

While our brief look at management roles has finished, the reality is that managers never stop learning these roles, and they add more roles all the time. Recognize that every manager will go through his or her own developmental struggles in learning to manage and lead in a 21st century organization. It is clear that to be successful in dealing with real-world management challenges, you must not only develop your skills and competencies in all the roles of management, but you must also be able to know when to draw upon each one. The situations, people, and problems/issues involved help direct managers to which approach or approaches might work best.

For example, if your organization is facing a structural change, such as that which occurs during downsizing, you will end up drawing upon your roles as Architect (in making sure you have grouping and linking mechanisms in place as the structure changes), as Politician (as you explain and ready employees for the change), as Leader (as you orchestrate and implement the changes), as Motivator (in rewarding the desired behaviors of those employees who are staying and praising the ones who are leaving), and as Coach (for employees who may need to take on different jobs or tasks and do not feel prepared to do so). As you encounter various situations and contexts in your managerial career, it is helpful to think about which of the roles you are being called to enact.

As we bring this brief look at managing in a 21st century organization to a close, let's summarize some of the most important lessons from the book that you need to remember as you develop your own managerial competencies. Following each one, I've provided a few ideas for improving and developing them.

Lesson #1: Managers who are the most successful at demonstrating emotional competence (both in understanding and managing their own emotions, as well as being able to read and respond to others' emotions, vocal cues, body language, and facial expressions) generally are seen as more trustworthy and as more effective leaders. Gaining the trust and respect of followers is paramount for implementing strategies and achieving the organization's goals, attracting and retaining qualified employees, and leading and managing organizational changes.

Developing Your Emotional Competence: Increased self-awareness allows us to recognize our feelings, and transforms us from merely reacting to stimuli to being able to create our own response. One strategy to develop better self-awareness is to practice *mindfulness.* One way mindfulness supports this is by decreasing our internal "noise" which can distract us and limit our attention and focus. There are several short and practical books on how to begin practicing mindfulness, as well as some free online classes. You might also find a class near where you live, too.

Better emotional self-management requires the ability to describe our feelings. In fact, recent research has revealed that being able to describe and name our feelings (e.g., "I feel very angry, so angry that I could throw a chair at that wall") can actually limit and sometimes reverse our emotional response by activating the cerebral cortex (the reasoning part of the brain).[1] This may be a large challenge for some people, but it has established benefits for slowing down our knee-jerk emotional and behavioral reactions.

Social awareness and relationship management are really all about understanding our own impact on others (i.e., how do our own behaviors and emotions affect another person?), as well as the impact of others' behaviors and emotions on us. Social awareness, first and foremost, requires *empathy*— the ability for us to see a situation or problem from someone else's perspective or to feel what another is feeling. Developing empathy takes practice; but the good news is that every time we meet another person we get a chance to practice our empathic skills.

Listening deeply is another skill that is important in developing emotional competence, as it helps in constructive conflict resolution, evaluating, coaching, and working collaboratively with others. Focusing on what another says and how they say it sends the message that you "hear" them and their concerns.

Remember that developing your emotional competence is a life-long journey, but as you get better at it, relationships will improve, and you will develop

---

[1] Torre, J.B. and Lieberman, M.D. (2018). Putting feelings into words: Affect labeling as implicit emotion regulation *Emotion Review,* 10, 2, 116–124. https://doi.org/10.1177/1754073917742706

more confidence and trust in your own emotions and how you manage them. It will also help you develop the interpersonal charisma that is important for leaders as they persuade their followers to implement important organizational changes.

Lesson #2: Successful problem-solving requires managers to deal with the root causes of problems, not merely the symptoms, and to provide employees with opportunities to come up with creative solutions for addressing those problems. Being aware of and using all the "lenses" (i.e., strategic design, political, and cultural) will give managers different insights into what potential root causes may be, allowing them to focus more directly on specific strategies for dealing with organizational problems.

Developing Your Problem-solving Competence: There are several ways to improve your ability to analyze causes and come up with solutions or ways to manage problems. Remember that solving problems requires both analytic and creative skills. If you have recognized that you need more practice and development in logic, analysis, and strategic thinking, try playing some games that require those skills, e.g., Sudoku, chess, bridge, or puzzles. For example, here is a classic logic puzzle that will see how logical and analytical you are. It is a version of a puzzle that was supposedly developed by Albert Einstein.[2]

Who Owns the Shark?

- There are five adjoining houses in a row in different colors: blue, green, red, white and yellow.
- In each house lives a person of different nationality: British, Indonesian, German, American and Dutch.
- Each person drinks a different beverage: grape juice, coffee, milk, tea and water.
- Each person has a different job: journalist, postman, magician, astronaut and actuary.
- Each person keeps a different pet: tiger, zebra, parrot, shark and aardvark.

The following constraints to the "problem" are listed below:

- The British person lives in a red house.
- The Dutch person keeps an aardvark.
- The Indonesian drinks tea.
- The green house is on the left of the white, next to it.

---

[2] Source: Logic Puzzle developed by Albert Einstein.

- The owner of the green house drinks coffee.
- The journalist rears parrots.
- The owner of the yellow house is an actuary.
- The person living in the house in the center drinks milk.
- The American lives in the first house.
- The astronaut lives next to the person who owns a tiger.
- The man who keeps a zebra lives next to the actuary.
- The postman drinks grape juice.
- The German is a magician.
- The American lives next to the blue house.
- The astronaut has a neighbor who drinks water.

The question you must answer is "Who owns the shark?" The answer is at the very end of this chapter; but don't look until you've tried solving it yourself!

Some of you reading this book may be very logical and analytical, but you may need to develop your creativity. Developing creativity means exercising the right side of your brain and developing your imagination. Listed below are some ideas for exercising your creative ability:

- Seek out creative people. Creative people tend to have the power to see what might be, so associating with them will likely spark new ideas and ways of looking at things. Look for people who are fun to talk to and come from different disciplines, backgrounds, cultures and experiences. They can help you to see things from different perspectives and develop your imagination.
- Associate more with pre-school children. Young children are the most ideal to mix with, as they generally use both sides of their brains. Their world is filled with fantasy, and yours can be, too, if you explore their world and how they see simple, everyday things.
- Try your hand at writing short stories or poetry, as they can unleash new ways of seeing thinking about things. Drawing or painting can do the same thing.
- Read more and in different genres. If you are used to reading non-fiction (like this book!), try reading mysteries or other fiction. Make up your own endings to short stories. Look at cookbooks and try to improve on the recipes with your own ingredients and ideas.

Lesson #3: Like all people, managers have needs, biases, and schema that can impede their objectivity surrounding people and situations. It is crucial that managers recognize what those are and how they might influence their decision-making processes and outcomes. And while managers may not be able to completely eliminate their biases, the ability to recognize when they are getting in the way of making appropriate and necessary decisions is crucial for gaining employee trust, particularly when difficult and complex decisions are required.

Developing Your Decision-making Competence. As we have already discussed, the decisions we make often have underlying needs (like control and approval) that drive them, and these are very difficult to overcome, primarily because they are deep-seated from our earliest experiences. But some decisions we make are due to unconscious biases and prejudices. Since unconscious biases are not permanent, they are malleable and can be changed by devoting intention, attention, and time to developing new associations. It involves taking the time to consciously think about possible biases prior to making decisions.[3]

Here are a few ideas you might try to become more aware of your decision-making biases and prejudices:

- Like the previous suggestions for developing emotional competence, improving our empathy and practicing perspective-taking on issues also helps us recognize if or when we may be engaging in unconscious bias toward someone or some issue.
- If you think you may not be as objective as you need to be, bring in another person to your decision-making process. Sometimes he or she can provide a check on your own opinions or perceptions.
- Be aware of contexts or situations that tend to trigger your biases. For example, in hiring employees, do you tend to associate a particular positive (or negative) characteristic demonstrated by a potential candidate with a previous employee who was successful (or unsuccessful)?

Lesson #4: Although managers do not directly motivate employees, they have a crucial role to play in creating an environment in which employees want to do their best work. Providing support, clearing barriers that impede employees from doing their jobs well, holding them accountable for implementing agreed-upon solutions or behavioral changes, and making sure that desired behaviors and outcomes are rewarded appropriately goes a long way in increasing employees' motivation and productivity. Providing a motivating, challenging workplace in which employees feel supported and valued is one of the primary reasons people will want to work for and with you.

---

[3] Blair, I.V. (2002). The malleability of automatic stereotypes and prejudice. *Personnel and Social Psychology Review,* 6, 242–61.

Developing Your Competency in Encouraging and Rewarding Others:
One thing all managers need to recognize is that people are more apt to be
motivated when they can see how their efforts effect the big picture. To that
end, work on developing an understanding of the core values that drive the
organization, and then help employees make the connection with their own
values. If you are able to have them see how their own personal values and
contribution fit into the overall organization, they will respond more positively and more productively.

As we've already discussed, people need to feel appreciated and valued.
However, you must discover how your employees feel most appreciated. In
their best-selling book, *The 5 Languages of Appreciation in the Workplace*,
Chapman and White discuss five different ways people want to receive
appreciation: words of affirmation, quality time, acts of service, tangible gifts
and rewards, and physical touch (in the workplace, more like handshakes,
brief and appropriate hugs, high fives, and fist bumps). The premise of the
book is that the mismatch of what a manager values as appreciation and what
her direct report values doesn't produce the intended reaction. For example,
as a manager, if you believe that your subordinate would value public affirmation for completion of a successful project, but the subordinate feels utterly
mortified to be acknowledged in public, she will not feel appreciated at all.
Choosing ways to show appreciation that are based on your own value or
"love language" won't work and may often create relational tension between
you and your direct reports. Figuring out what really shows your appreciation
in ways that your employees will feel appreciated is not difficult, but it does
take some effort to learn their preferences. If you are interested in learning
more about how to apply the five languages of appreciation in your workplace,
and taking the inventory to see what your appreciation "language" is, the
book by Gary Chapman and Paul White is a good one.[4]

Finally, to create a motivational environment for employees, managers
need to be able to focus on engaging them in solving the real problems and
issues they face. One way to do this is to develop a capacity to shift perspective and ask different questions. For example if you are asking what is wrong
with a situation, also ask what is right. If you dwell on employees challenges,
start focusing on their strengths. If you are trying to understand something
in the past, switch to how it affects the present or the future. If you are asking
how something occurred, you might change it to *why* it occurred. This gives

---

[4]Chapman, G. D., & White, P. E. (2012). *The 5 languages of appreciation in the
workplace: Empowering organizations by encouraging people.* Revised and updated.
Chicago: Northfield Publishing.

both you and your employees a new way of looking at situations and may spark some very creative solutions. Of course, as we have already discussed, the ability to see problems and issues differently is the hallmark of a good manager, and developing this competency is one that will serve you well for your entire career.

Lesson #5: Managers play one of the most important roles in employee development, both in evaluating the strengths, challenges, and competencies of employees, as well as in helping them to develop both personally and professionally. Managers who see employee development as an investment, rather than as an expense, are much more likely to attract and retain high potential employees. It gives your organization a huge competitive advantage, too, because while competitors can replicate products, price, quality, and delivery times, they can never replicate your employees!

Developing Your Competency in Evaluating and Coaching Others: As we discussed in the chapters, "Manager as Evaluator" and "Manager as Coach," part of the requirements to be effective in those roles is to be able to be present and deeply listen to your employees. For some people, that is a challenge, particularly in our fast-paced, chaotic workplaces and with our ever-present communication devices. But the ability to focus on the other person is key to good coaching, as well as providing constructive and challenging feedback. To help improve your ability to be present to others, try this:

1. Think about a person with whom you've had a miscommunication or a disagreement. It could your boss, a direct report, a peer, or a customer. It could also be with a family member or friend with whom you are struggling to regain a positive relationship.
2. Schedule a meeting in which you intentionally ask real, open-ended questions and make eye contact as you ask them. Concentrate on hearing what the other person says, and watch their body language and facial expression as they say it.
3. At the end of your meeting, ask them how you could be helpful to them, and thank them for meeting with you.
4. Follow up in a few days to see if they have further questions, comments, or suggestions on what you talked about.

As we develop our ability to connect with others, we also improve our comfort level with providing feedback and coaching. The more authentically we can relate to our employees, the more they will trust that our suggestions and help are truly given in the spirit of helping them to become their best selves.

The Bottom Line

All of us can get better in all the roles we play—whether they are parental roles, teaching roles, or managerial roles. I hope that this book has given you some new ideas about how you can continue to develop your own managerial competencies. And, most importantly, I wish you every success in your careers and every happiness in your lives.

Solution to the logic puzzle

House:	Yellow	Blue	Red	Green	White
Nationality:	American	Indonesian	British	German	Dutch
Drink:	Water	Tea	Milk	Coffee	Grape Juice
Pet:	Tiger	Zebra	Parrot	**SHARK**	Aardvark
Occupation:	Actuary	Astronaut	Journalist	Magician	Postman

Index